11

RAY REARDON

Ray Reardon
with Peter Buxton

David & Charles
Newton Abbot   London   North Pomfret (Vt)

British Library Cataloguing in Publication Data

Reardon, Ray
  Ray Reardon
  1. Reardon, Ray 2. Snooker players – Wales – Biography
  I. Title II. Buxton, Peter
  794.7'35'0924 GV900.S6
  ISBN 0 7153 8262 4

Typeset by ABM Typographics Limited, Hull
and printed in Great Britain
by Butler & Tanner, Frome
for David & Charles (Publishers) Limited
Brunel House   Newton Abbot   Devon

Published in the United States of America
by David & Charles Inc
North Pomfret   Vermont 05053   USA

CONTENTS

1
PENNILESS CHAMPION

*There is a tide in the affairs of men, which, taken at the flood, leads
on to fortune* Shakespeare

Down went the last black and I was snooker champion of the
world, eighteen months after becoming a full-time professional
and with exactly eight pounds in my bank account. Not that the
eight pounds meant much, for I could not even have competed
in the championships if I had not been able to borrow £100 from
a miner friend of my father's.

To reach that position of grinding insolvency I had spent
twelve of my thirty-eight years in the coalmining industry in
South Wales and North Staffordshire and almost eight years as
a policeman, before deciding to try to earn a living with my
snooker cue and I make no secret of the fact that there had been
times when my mind was filled with doubt.

There was never any question on the score of my ability, for I
had plenty of confidence in myself and I knew what I could do,
but occasionally the financial struggle to get established at a
time when the snooker row was very hard to hoe made me
wonder if it was all worthwhile and whether it would not be
better to look for another job to restore the family's security.

Any lingering fears flew out of the window on that magic
night when I won the world crown by beating John Pulman 39-
34 in the 1970 final at the Victoria Hall, Bloomsbury Square,
London. It was an unforgettable experience and though I did
not realise at the time the extent to which my gamble on the
future had paid off, it was the turning point of my life. Snooker
was approaching its floodtide and I found myself riding the
crest of the biggest wave.

My victory in the first Pot Black tournament was already in the can before the world championships began and BBC-2 television's practice of filming it in advance in one continuous sudden-death competition, then splitting it into weekly episodes, was very much to my advantage. The series was not shown until the summer, when I was on the holiday camp circuit, so that the world title and weekly exposure on the box combined to give me wonderful publicity and to draw the crowds to see me in action.

That was not the only stroke of luck, for it all happened at a time when snooker was beginning to benefit from the bingo craze, which generated income that revitalised clubs up and down the country. Oddly enough, when the bingo boom first started a lot of club committees decided that snooker tables were too costly to maintain and took up too much floor space, so they had them cleared out. By the time the clubs decided to invest their newly-acquired wealth in bigger and better premises, their members were demanding something more than bingo, so that snooker and concert rooms were included in the plans.

This in turn meant that when colour television triggered off a nationwide interest in snooker, there were some very good facilities available all over Britain. I was fortunate to strike the top at the right time. Soon more engagements came flooding in than it was physically possible to accept, though I did my best. It was not long before I was out of single figures at the bank.

'Eyes Down' for bingo meant a full house for me. I am grateful, too, for television's love affair with snooker. The game had been forced to survive for a good many years in the face of almost total neglect by the media and still had, at the lower end of the scale, an aura of social and moral degeneracy.

Snooker and the television cameras were made for each other and their marriage transformed my life as best man, besides giving birth to a new generation of prosperous players. It turned all our cues into magic wands.

Let it be said that the marriage was not without its teething troubles. Some thirteen years or so ago both channels were televising challenge matches involving five frames and they let it be

8

known that ideally the score should be 2-2, so that the programme could work up into a thrilling finish.

Various top players were involved in this series and it is not to be thought that they had anything but the best intentions or that producers issued instructions to them, but everyone was well aware that if the matches were not good television the series would not last long or be repeated. They acted in the best interests of the game as they saw them, but before long it was realised that snooker was following professional wrestling over the border from sport to entertainment.

Officials of the Billiards Association and Control Council recognised that the final score of 3-2 or 4-3 was recurring so often that the coincidence went beyond mere chance. Even worse, there were occasions when in order to keep it close, an in-form player had to go for ridiculous shots and throw away a frame. In some cases snookers had to be edited from a match so that the programme would be of the required length, yet finish with a winner and a loser.

The money from television was important to the Control Council and even the amateurs were glad of the perks, for there were £10 clothing vouchers, free travel, meals and accommodation, yet there were still complaints about 'fixing' matches, of forfeiting public confidence and denying snooker's validity as a public spectacle.

All this seems a long time ago now. Those who thought the game was being ruined by the intrusion and demands of the cameras were vastly outnumbered by those who glimpsed the possibilities of colour television. A greater expertise was developed in presenting the sport on the small screen and it soon became clear that the game was compelling viewing for millions of people. By 1985 the prize-money in the game will total something like £2,000,000 a year and it is still rising.

A boy's will is the wind's will   Longfellow

My love for snooker goes back to my childhood in Tredegar, Monmouthshire, now Gwent, the South Wales town of some

24,000 souls where I was born on 8 October 1932, into an environment that ensured coalpits and snooker would loom large in my life.

According to my father, Ben, there were times when it seemed decidedly unlikely that I would reach my third birthday and that was not because I was a sickly baby. The problem was that Mr and Mrs Reardon's first little blessing was a classic case of do-it-yourself insomnia. It seems that during the first two years of my life I slept when I should have been awake and cried when I should have been asleep, which made it tough on my mother and father, especially Ben, who of course was working at the pit.

The danger to me was that he used to fall asleep while nursing me on his knee and might easily have dropped me accidentally. The much more serious danger, he tells me, was that there were times when my crying brought him the strong temptation to bung me out of the window. According to Ben I kept them awake so much that at times they were literally walking in their sleep, but fortunately it does not seem to have done either of us much harm. Mind you, it does not seem to console him much when I tell him I sleep all right now.

There is in Tredegar a clock that stands proudly in the town centre. Its hands showed 3.45 in the afternoon on a day when I was in a crocodile of children who were returning somewhat unwillingly to school from the funeral of Headmaster Sparks.

He had lived on the other side of Tredegar from Georgetown Secondary School and we had been to pay our last respects to a man who during his years of service had influenced the community more than most. I did not mind attending the funeral service, but I must confess that 3.45 seemed to me to be just a little bit on the late side for us to be going back to school. What appealed much more strongly to me were the snooker tables on the premises of the Tredegar Workmen's Institute Society that were attracting me like a magnet from across the road. So I slipped quietly out of the shuffling column and dodged between the cars and lorries to challenge Tommy Biggs, the manager with a wooden leg.

'Hello Young Banger,' said Tommy, who had lost a leg in an accident when jumping from a moving train on his way home from work at the Pochin Colliery, just down the valley. My father, Ben, was nicknamed Banger when he played in the forward line for Tredegar Town football team and I was automatically dubbed the younger version, in accordance with the general practice.

Things were usually very quiet at the institute in the late afternoon in midweek and Tommy Biggs was just hanging about with nothing to do, so he readily agreed to give me 15 points start for sixpence (2½p) of my pocket-money. I had just won the frame when the door of the institute swung open and there stood my maths teacher, Ivor Jimmy Jones.

'Didn't know he should still have been at school,' said Tommy Biggs, who was no mean opportunist, for by getting off the mark first with those few words he sidestepped for ever the question of paying me the sixpence I had just won. Instead of getting the money I was marched off smartly back to school, where I was warned in no uncertain terms to mend my ways.

I was nearing my seventh birthday when World War II broke out and for most of the time it seemed remote from our valley, except for one night when I heard a bomb drop on a hillside, well away from its intended target, which was the steelworks at Ebbw Vale.

I was soon to discover in a painful way that I possessed a much greater degree of accuracy than that German aircrew, for one of my minor misdemeanours earned me six of the best for the flukiest shot of my life, to that point, at least.

Pea-shooters were all the rage at the time in Tredegar and elsewhere in South Wales and we were fortunate to have on hand plenty of reeds of suitable size, which meant that we did not have to spend our precious pocket-money on the shop version. One day I spotted a good target as we were filing into school, but the snag was that Elwyn Jones turned his head at the crucial moment and the berry I was using as a missile went straight into his ear, as accurately as I can sink an easy black.

There was no applause from Headmaster Sparks for my pea-

11

shooter virtuosity, only three strokes of the cane on each hand before the whole school at morning assembly. They did not even give me the berry back when they got it out of his ear.

That was one of the few occasions when my brushes with authority had nothing to do with snooker. I had not reached my teens when someone reported to my father, 'Ben, your Ray is up at the institute, playing for money.' I still do not know whether he was more worried about my playing for money, or losing money to someone taking advantage of my tender years, but my father was soon at the institute confronting me.

'How much have you lost?' he demanded. I was able to tell him that I was, in fact, in pocket. He thought for a moment or so, then said, 'You would win more if you kept your head down and held the cue properly.' He still tells me off for lifting my head, even as recently as the 1981 championships, and he is as right now as he was then, when four defeats at sixpence a time accounted for a whole week's pocket-money.

A billiard ball figured in one of the worst tricks I can remember, involving a lad named Archie, who was never destined to become the Brain of Britain. Someone started an argument that it was impossible to get a billiard ball into the human mouth, which may have been a simple opinion, put forward without guile, or the motive may have been a good deal less innocent. Anyway, Archie promptly proved the statement to be unfounded.

Since those days I have met one or two people I am convinced would have been able to do this trick without any difficulty at all had they chosen to try it, but Archie was not in their class when it came to the size of the mouth. All the unfortunate Archie proved was that he could get a billiard ball into his mouth and he could not get it out again. We had to parade him through the streets of Tredegar, comprehensively snookered, until at hospital they removed enough of his teeth to make way for his next meal, which he ate with difficulty. It seemed a lot funnier at the time than it does now, I think.

We were high spirited, but those of us whose interests were centred on the snooker table were not badly behaved, in fact I can only remember one instance when things got out of hand. It involved a lad who needed to pot the black to win and missed it, which annoyed him so much that he picked up the ball and slung it through a window that happened to be closed at the time. I cannot remember whether there was any money on the game, but in any case he got a bill for the replacement of the window and a year's ban from the premises, which guaranteed that nobody else stepped out of line.

Come to think of it, snooker has never had any problems with hooliganism in my recollection. I have known deadly rivals to exchange blows on the odd occasion and an instance when a business changed hands on the outcome of a game, but you rarely hear of the police being called to a snooker hall. In my experience they pay the occasional routine visit and that is all.

There are a lot of people today who are out of work, including a lot of youngsters who have nothing to do that attracts them and does not upset others. I do not want to get involved here in the rights and wrongs of the situation, but I cannot see things changing to any great extent and I can see snooker as an inexpensive leisure activity that a lot of people enjoy.

Efforts have been made within the sport to spread the boundaries and for the last twelve years the Billiards and Snooker Foundation has attempted to work through local authorities and youth clubs in an effort to reach boys and girls of school age, offering coaching to an advanced level.

The Foundation was formed on the lines of those serving golf and lawn tennis. Trade members contribute a fixed proportion of their turnover to finance the work, which is also grant-aided on a modest scale. Snooker is included in the Duke of Edinburgh's Award scheme.

Much has been done, but there is always scope for more. There are more and better facilities now and standards generally have been raised, but snooker is not a game for which provision is automatically made at youth clubs and leisure centres, even though it is attractive to both sexes and to people of all ages, from the young to those who can no longer cope with more physically demanding sports.

Voluntary help or sponsorship is still needed to help individuals and teams to compete abroad. These are all areas in which development could take place to the advantage of a community with time on its hands.

I admit to having a vested interested in the matter, but I do believe more snooker facilities will have to come into the picture when the government starts to think seriously about what people are going to do during the hours when, in the past, they would have been working.

Historians relate what they would have believed
Benjamin Franklin

Now that snooker commands a world-wide audience it is not unusual to hear people talking about the game's working-class background. They do so in error. It seems that a central figure in the development of the modern game in the mid-1880s was Field Marshal Sir Neville Bowles Chamberlain, formerly of the Devonshire Regiment, who upon retirement from the British Army took up an advisory post with the Indian Army. He was at a station in the Nilgiri Hills in Southern India and at a time when everyone was bored in the heat of the summer he devised a new game that was a combination of billiards, pyramids, black pool and life pool. He added the coloured balls to the existing fifteen reds and a black.

From the start it was the practice to play a red, then a colour and soon, while playing in the Ooty Club, Sir Neville found that the cue ball had been left behind a colour and he was prevented from playing the next red, as required. This could not have been a tactful thing to do to a Field Marshal of such distinction, especially in the heat of the summer, whether by design or accident. Sir Neville turned purple-faced to his wretched opponent and called him a 'snooker'. This was a derisive term for a first-year cadet at the Royal Military Academy in Woolwich. The word seems to have been derived from the verb *snoke*, which meant to sneak about, as no doubt new cadets did at first at the famous academy where harsh penalties awaited the rash.

In out-of-school hours we usually played on the slopes of the Dommon Mountain on the Ebbw Vale side of Tredegar. Our house backed on to the lower slopes and we used to slide down the one-in-four gradient using a piece of cardboard as a toboggan. You can go pretty fast down there, I can tell you, for I remember that once I was caught by a piece of wire stuck in the ground and it sent me base over apex, breaking my left arm.

I was not accident prone and the only other injury of note I can recall involved an old bicycle we were trying to restore to working order. It was in the house, standing upside down on its saddle and handlebars. With one hand I was making the pedals whiz round and I was careless enough to get the fourth finger on my other hand, the right, caught between the gearwheel and the chain, which left the fingertip hanging off and caused my mother to faint.

We had a neighbour who was a great one in an emergency and she came to my aid with more willingness and enthusiasm than skill, slapping on some ointment and binding up my finger before despatching me to hospital. By the time I got there and reached my turn to see the doctor the ointment she had used had turned into an early version of super-glue. It required a long and painful struggle to remove the binding and allow the doctor to stitch on my fingertip properly. Evidence of his skill is there to see after more than forty years.

My young life was subject to quite a lot of civilising influences, which is no more than you would expect in Wales. Inevitably music was one, and when I was about six I started to learn to play the cornet at the Salvation Army hall. Judging by those early experiences I never did have any natural talent for blowing my own trumpet and my efforts at singing were no more successful. I shared the widely held view that every Welshman is born with a fine singing voice, but when I sang at school I produced on the face of my poor music teacher expressions that I later realised were suppressed horror. They sent me to another classroom to read a book. In my teens I joined a glee club, but they soon found out where the noise was coming from and invited me to leave.

19

Oh, the wild joys of living! The leaping from rock up to rock, the strong rending of boughs from the fir-tree, the cool silver shock of the plunge in a pool's living water   Robert Browning

My musical shortcomings did not weigh heavily upon me, for I was more at home on the mountainside, where we used to drink from a spring of ice cold ironwater. This water, the common enemy of the ironstone mine, was reddish brown in colour and tasted bitter, but we believed it was clean and we came to no harm. Certainly we were in no danger from anaemia.

We ran as wild as the wild ponies on that mountainside. The ponies were free, except when we caught one with an improvised lasso as we had seen the cowboys do in films. We would ride the pony bareback, jeering at the perspiring bobby on a bike who had been sent to catch us. Years later I was to learn exactly how he felt on gradients of that kind, for I, too, had to ride one of those police bicycles and it was like a piece of heavy wrought iron with hoops attached.

We dug our own den out of the hillside and roofed it in with planks. It was the centre of our private world. We took care of our voracious appetites by roasting potatoes in the hot ashes of an open fire and nothing ever tasted better, despite the inevitable garnishing of soil and charcoal. To supplement our al fresco diet we ate raw carrots and any other vegetables we could acquire.

Money hardly ever figured in our lives at all, for there was not enough of it about to matter, but we did have a lot of fun, especially as our interest in girls developed and we devised our own games down by the river and tried to avoid crowds of more than two. As the French say, 'Vive la différence!'

One of the other joys in my life was swimming. I went with Brian Smith every day to the open air baths in Bedwellty Park, from the time the baths opened in early May until they closed in September, no matter what the weather or temperature. Some days the thermometer showed only 54°F in and out of the water, which most people would find distinctly cool.

My Uncle John was wicket keeper and opening bat for the

Whether it was delight at the effect the incident had on Sir Neville that formed the attraction, or a sadistic pleasure in frustrating an opponent is not certain, but the tactic and the name 'snooker' were adopted for the game.

Things moved a stage further when Sir Neville met John Roberts, junior, the professional billiards champion, whose father had also been a great player. This John Roberts seems to have been to billiards what Dr W. G. Grace was to cricket and this dominant personality began to push the new game of snooker commercially in the late 1880s. In 1891 John Dowland drew up the first set of rules, since various local versions had been developed in places to which the game had spread from India. Dowland is described as 'a minor professional' and this may have been the case, or it could have been because some people at the time thought him an upstart. No matter, for he helped to establish the game, which flourished in big homes, clubs and hotels, until Joe Davis became the hero of the High Street snooker halls.

In the nineteenth century cue could also mean to swindle on credit, but I am sure that has nothing to do with snooker.

2
BOYHOOD TREATS

What hunger is to food, zest is to life   Bertrand Russell

Billiards, not snooker, was the main game in my early years in Tredegar, the first three of which were spent at 10 Inkerman Street, after which we went to live at the home of my maternal grandmother, Gertrude Jenkins, at 48 High Street.

My mouth still waters when I think of my grandmother's baking. She made wonderful pikelets and Welsh cakes on her bakestone, while her non-greasy doughnuts were superb and her pancakes unbelievable. I make allowances for the legendary appetite of the growing, healthy lad, for I was one of those people who could 'eat a horse and chase the jockey', but I have still to come across anyone who could make chips to match those produced by my grandmother. Perhaps it is just that the tastebuds wither, but that food provided magical treats in my boyhood.

Oddly enough, I can rarely remember seeing her enjoy her own baking. She ate very little, living for most of the time on bread and butter, with perhaps an orange or a small portion of fish. She may have been feeding me up for the hard, physical work that lay ahead, for ours was a male-oriented society, but I can say with certainty that if she made sacrifices on my behalf they were never met with ingratitude.

My first school was Earl Street Infants and it could be reached by two routes from our house. It must have taken me some time to get used to school, for when I was about five my mother took me there by one route and when she got back home I had beaten her to it, using the other streets. When I was eight we moved to Whitworth Terrace.

16

(*Above*) My first match with the legendary Joe Davis in 1957 at the Ash Bank Country Club, Stoke-on-Trent. (*Below*) Wedding day on Easter Monday 1959. Sue and I leave the church beneath an arch of cues

(*Right*) A study in
determination. My earliest
picture in the family album

(*Below*) With Jack Carney in
London for the all-Welsh
final of the British Youths'
championship in 1950

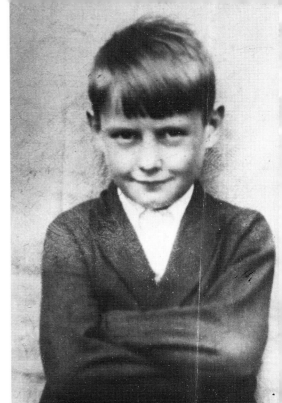

YMCA cricket team and I played for them, too, fielding close to the wicket and batting halfway down the order. My reflexes and co-ordination were pretty good.

Rugby Union football is a game with great traditions in Wales, as everyone knows, and I tried it at school. One incident still stands out in my memory, when I was running down the wing and a lad named Keith was cutting across to tackle me. As he reached me I checked my stride and he hurtled past me with such force that his head got stuck in some iron railings that stood on that side of the pitch. He must have achieved a fair velocity, for the school had to call on the local firemen to free him. Keith went on to qualify and practise as a doctor and the last time I saw him I noticed that he still holds his head at an awkward angle.

Significantly, I suppose, my preference was for a round ball game and I had a trial at right-half in the town's schoolboy football team, but there were about fifty-nine others taking part in that game and no one got much chance to shine. I did not catch the eye of the selectors, as they say, but I have always enjoyed my football.

Teaching is the art of awakening the natural curiosity of young minds Anatole France

Outdoor pursuits always took second place to the billiard table. My father, Ben, was the National Union of Mineworkers' leader at the Ty Trist Colliery and was also a member of the institute committee. He has an older brother, Dan, and three younger brothers, Ray, John and Bryn. They are all handy with a cue and they played both billiards and snooker for the institute teams.

Uncle Dan, who lived with us and did not marry until he was in his mid-forties, first guided me into their footsteps when I was about eight. On a Sunday afternoon he would set up a game on the kitchen table, using books to form pockets, a miniature cue and marbles made from Tizer bottle tops to serve as balls.

As a Christmas present my mother bought me a billiard table top to put on the kitchen table. It measured 4ft by 2ft, though until I got involved in the manufacture of tables I always thought it was bigger. It seemed bigger to me when I was that age.

Uncle Dan was a railway worker and he also played chess for the Monmouthshire county team. He was a devotee of grand-masters Reti, Morphy and Alekhine and he took part in postal matches with some of the top players. After the family lunch on a Sunday he would start work on his chess problems and I would set up the billiard table in the kitchen. Uncle Dan could never resist for long, for he could hear me playing and soon he would poke his head round the door and say, 'I suppose I could take you on for a game.' He would then play by the hour.

I was even keener than he was and I would play whenever I could, morning, afternoon and night, even roping in Dan's wife, Aunty Lena. When I was nine or ten Dad started to take me to the institute once a week. At first Tom Ball was caretaker-manager, then Tommy Biggs took over as manager and though you were not supposed to go into the institute until you were fourteen, they allowed me in on Thursday from 4 pm to 6 pm, or until members started to arrive. We were allowed to use tables one or two, which were out of the way, but if anyone wanted the table on which I was playing I had to pack up. Though I was not very big then, I still had to play properly. There was no climbing on the table to play a shot, so I soon learned to use the rest.

It was from that institute that the road took me to six world championships and I will never cease to be grateful for the chance I was given there to develop my skill. These were truly billiard tables and potting was slightly more difficult than it is now because the mouth of the pocket was altered slightly as snooker became the more popular game.

The institute was paid for by the union members and the colliery owners and it incorporated a library and a cinema, where seats cost less than they did elsewhere. My favourite table, No 4, is still there, but things have worsened over the years. Now the institute is a licensed club and pit closures have brought hard times. A year or so ago I was joined by Terry Griffiths, another Welshman to become world professional snooker champion, and together we raised £3,000 for restoration work at the institute. It was the least I could do.

When I was only twelve I played in the Welsh boys' snooker championship and we had quite a family outing to the match at Oakdale Miners' Institute, where I was defeated. A year later, though I was still twelve months under the minimum age at which I should have been admitted to the Tredegar institute, I was tall enough to get away with playing for the team, along with my father and three of his brothers, Bryn being away serving as a petty officer in the Royal Navy. We played in the Sirhowy Valley Billiards and Snooker League. There were eight in a team and usually four tables were in use, with each man playing two games.

When I moved to North Staffordshire I found that in the league there things were different, with only five in a team and each man playing only one game, which I think is a bit of a waste of time when you devote a whole night to the fixture.

When I was playing billiards I used to pile up breaks of 500 and 600, though not in championship conditions. I was always trying to win. In one Christmas handicap in Tredegar I met a prominent local man named Tom Jones, who had played in the same football team as my Dad. Just to avoid confusion, he did not become famous as a singer.

His match with me was a close one and I needed only two to win, with his ball left near a pocket. I put it down without hesitation, Christmas spirit or not, and that really put the cat among the pigeons. Tom Jones took such a poor view of what I had done that he would not shake hands with me and, in fact, never spoke to me for the next four months. Though I had done nothing against the rules, for one reason or another it has always been regarded as a sign of a serious character defect if you pot your opponent's ball, the act of a bounder and a cad. I do not see it that way and I cannot remember any member of my family voicing an objection.

23

Oddly enough, in Stoke-on-Trent some years later, one of my friends and most loyal supporters, Jack Window, found himself in exactly the same position in a league match. He refused to pot the white ball and his team was beaten. They gave him a bad time.

There have been rows in a number of sports about so-called unsporting actions that are not specifically outlawed by the rules, but breach them in spirit, or so it is claimed. There was one celebrated incident in cricket when the batting side needed a six off the last ball to win and it was bowled under-arm, to reduce the odds to nil. Whatever the merits of that particular argument, I cannot see how potting a billiard ball in a perfectly normal manner that is catered for in the system of scoring can possibly be described as unfair.

It's them that take advantage that get advantage i' this world
George Eliot

There are those in Tredegar who would never have dreamed of giving a sucker an even break and most of them were familiar with the Lucania snooker hall on the other side of town, about half a mile from the miners' institute. A lot of steelworkers, including current professional Cliff Wilson, used to haunt the Lucania and that was where the real gambling was done, for among the clientele were quite a few hustlers like Charlie (The Shark) Smith, a crafty player who would not have been out of place in a Damon Runyon story about the characters on Broadway, apart from his accent.

Most of the action at the Lucania took place on a Saturday and you had to be there early to find a place in the hall. It was particularly hectic and fruitful in the afternoons, after the pubs had shut. When I was in my mid-teens I could make £3 or £4 on a Saturday at the Lucania and that was a lot of money in those days, equal to the wage for a week's work. The game I used to play to supplement my pocket-money so handsomely was skittles pool, with fourteen or fifteen players taking part at sixpence a time.

24

We played with three billiard balls and twelve skittles, ten white and two black, all of which were placed at specified points on the table. The game was 31 up and anyone who exceeded 31 lost a 'life', but could buy another. Numbers were drawn from a bag to decide the order of play.

The man who drew no 1 played the white ball or the spot white ball out of baulk, aiming for the red, which he had to strike first before hitting a skittle in order to score. No 2 played the remaining ball out of baulk, at either of the other two. The spot and plain white ball were used alternately as the cue ball, but every time you had to hit a ball, then a skittle.

You scored the value of the skittle you knocked down, with the exception of the black skittles. If you knocked one of them down you lost a 'life', but could purchase another. This could happen any number of times, as long as you said you were buying before the next player took his shot. However, when you bought another 'life' you started again with no points.

When a skittle was knocked down, it was replaced before the next player had his turn. If a ball was occupying its place, the ball was replaced on its own spot, as at the start of the game. There were other minor rules, but that is the general picture of this gambling game, which involved a certain amount of bluff, for if the others guessed the number you needed they would leave you in an impossible position.

The money was all put into a pocket, that is the starting stake and that used to buy new 'lives'. The winner scooped the pool.

To be successful you had to develop a good working knowledge of angles. One variation used to develop this skill was to stick a pin in the pink spot and try to knock this down, after first hitting another ball. Believe it or not, it is possible to snooker someone behind that tiny pin.

Challenge matches were often made, with Charlie the Shark holding the stake money, which could be as much as £5 a time. Before his death some years ago, when I was world champion, I visited Charlie in hospital. We talked a lot about those days at the Lucania and the games that were crucial enough financially to help prepare me for the big time.

3
FALSE START TO MY CAREER

A clean glove often hides a dirty hand   English Proverb

Though I was a member of a mining family, I did not go straight from school into the pits. We knew all about the working conditions and the dangers that are the daily companions of miners, to say nothing of the anti-social hours, to give shift work its modern term, and the uncertain future of the industry in our part of Wales. So not surprisingly I was pointed towards a different career as a motor mechanic.

My three or four months of employment at a local garage began with an initiation ceremony that involved daubing a most important and private part of me with axle grease. However, I would not have you think it was this indignity that curtailed my time among the spanners and pressure gauges. Neither was it the all-pervading and hateful smell of petrol, that took away the taste of my food and contrived to curb even my appetite.

My early departure from the garage was not even due to the grime and grease that became ingrained in my hands. This was something I really disliked and perhaps it is as well that I developed something amounting almost to a phobia about it, for nothing could look worse on television or in tournaments than a man playing snooker with soiled hands and dirty nails.

Digressing for a moment, this phobia caused me to become the only miner I ever heard of in South Wales or North Staffordshire to do his job underground wearing white canvas gloves that started out looking something like those sported by the referee of televised snooker. I got my leg pulled quite a bit as a result of wearing those gloves, as you can imagine, but I was determined to keep my hands in good condition for snooker, since they are very much on display when you are in action. Perhaps I had subconsciously registered this fact while watching snooker at the institute in my earliest days.

No, it was not the fear of spoiling my hands that caused me to pack in the job at the garage. The fact is that as an apprentice mechanic I got only ten shillings (or 50p) a week, for grinding valves and greasing, which is not much when you consider that my mates were getting more than £3 a week at the pits. The job did not leave me much time for snooker, either, so I left it without regrets. Perhaps it was as well, because to this day I am hopeless when it comes to car maintenance.

I applied to go into coalmining as a Bevin Boy and while I was waiting I worked on the surface at Ty Trist. When I was accepted for training I went for two days a week to the Oakdale Centre.

The rest of the week was spent helping a collier underground, hacking with a pick and handling a shovel. There was a basic wage of just over £3 week and the collier usually paid a bit of pocket-money if you worked hard. Some were more generous than others. At first I was with Ron Jones, a friend of my father, then I was with Ted Hooker, known as 'Ted the Scrat'. He worked like a beaver and expected everybody else to do likewise, but he paid out only a shilling or two in pocket-money, so I did not stick with him for long.

I had left school at fourteen and was still under fifteen when I went into the pit. I only worked days, on the loading shift as it was called, mostly because I wanted to have the time to do my snooker practice. I would not work noons and nights, though I do not suppose I could have maintained that position if it had not been for a certain amount of union support and my growing reputation as a snooker player, for I was champion of Wales when I was eighteen.

Even so, it meant getting up at 5 am every day and getting back home about 2 pm or so. There were no pithead baths, so we had to travel home in our dirt and bath in a tub in front of the fire. At least we were never short of coal.

27

Ty Trist was an old pit, nearing the end of its working life, so after a while I moved to Pochin Colliery, just down the valley.

People today always look amazed and even sceptical when I tell them that we had to buy our own equipment as colliers. A pickshaft cost 1s 3d (7p), a blade 9d (4p) and an axe 8s 6d (42½p).

Pickshafts had a special use for a game called bat and catty, which I later found was known in North Staffordshire as tipcat. A 'catty' was made by cutting a piece off the pickshaft and tapering it at each end. The remainder of the shaft was used as a club, or bat, and the skill lay in placing the catty on the ground, rapping one of the tapered ends smartly to make it airborne, then striking it cleanly in mid-air, knocking it as far as possible, often 100 yards or more. Working in the pits makes colliers strong in the arms, shoulders and back.

It also hardens the hands and my eyes are sharp, so I was often able to catch the viciously spinning catty when we played this game on the red shale pitch called the Red Ground, which lay halfway up the 1,350ft slope on the other side of the valley from my home. In many respects, bat and catty was similar to baseball. Runs were taken in an almost identical manner and the hitter was out if the catty was caught.

An appeaser is one who feeds a crocodile, hoping it will eat him last Winston Churchill

It was on the Red Ground that I had my first experience of fighting as an adult. We were returning home from the Pochin Colliery by train after work when an argument broke out with another collier. I cannot think now what it was all about, but the upshot was that we agreed to settle our differences at 5 pm, stripped to the waist and facing each other in a ring formed by our respective supporters, who did not mind the trek up to the Red Ground if there was some free entertainment there.

Though it was a bareknuckle confrontation, the Marquis of Queensberry Rules were otherwise strictly enforced, so that kicking, gouging, butting and other tactics of an objectionable nature were not allowed. Today I suspect they would be acceptable in this type of punch-up, always supposing that fairly formal occasions of this kind have not been superseded entirely by mob-handed muggings, but in any case in those days conduct like that was rated on a par with cowardice and would attract stigma, if not swift retribution.

In our case it had to be a fair fight until one of us cried, 'Enough'. It was my opponent who packed in after six rounds, whereupon we shook hands and all went down to the pub and got drunk. There was not the slightest ill-feeling.

I was still not quite old enough to drink in a pub legally, though no-one who did not know would have guessed. Somehow though, in those days drink did not seem to lead to the violence it causes now. Teenagers and young adults had inherited a very keen sense of fair play and they never ganged up on anyone. Serious offences that are commonplace in this country now were almost unheard of in my part of the world at that time.

He who knows nothing doubts nothing   Spanish Proverb

Like all young men there were times when we were restless and craved excitement. Going to Blackpool with the family for the annual holiday always made me feel unsettled afterwards, when I reached my late teens. A typical itchy-footed reaction to one such holiday was a mad weekend when a friend, John Ingram, went with me on a forty mile bus trip to Cardiff with the intention of joining the Merchant Navy. There was not a single ship in the pool when we got there, or my subsequent history might have been very different. As it was we were soon skint and were glad to jump the Milk Train back to Tredegar.

John Ingram was also with me when, with Brian Smith and another friend, we responded to a Royal Air Force advertisement that said they guaranteed to teach a trade to anyone who signed for three years. We were prepared to have a go and we travelled to Cardington, only to find there would be no trade unless we signed for five years.

That was enough for me. It was not the length of time that

29

bothered me, but I felt that an attempt had been made to cheat me and no amount of persuasion by the commanding officer, the padre or anyone else would make me change my mind. At the time I was snooker champion of Wales and they were keen to sign me, but I felt they had not been straightforward and I got my travel warrant and went back home. When I got there my father looked up from his tea and said, 'I told you he would not last a week.'

Brian Smith was my companion in another escapade, when we cycled off on a Sunday to the Gilwern Canal and hired a rowing boat. We had taken a couple of drinks and it seemed like a good idea to make a play for two girls we saw on the towpath. In the course of the inevitable clowning we overturned the boat and had to ride home soaking wet, which did not amuse my mother.

When I was in my mid-teens my father decided he would do some alterations and concreting at home. The job involved moving quite a large quantity of bricks and other debris to a dump some distance away, so John Ingram and I offered to do the labouring for the princely sum of ten shillings (50p), a deal my father accepted with some quite obvious misgivings.

We had one wheelbarrow and we borrowed another from a neighbour a little further down the street. We were both enthusiastic and impatient, a calamitous combination in those circumstances and the inevitable result was that we broke the handle of the neighbour's barrow. We switched to using buckets to shift the rubble and predictably enough they were not up to the strain and the bottoms fell out. By this time my father was not exactly classing us as a help. He restrained himself from using any of the first words that came into his head, yet still managed to indicate firmly that he wished us to go away, which we did, triumphantly bearing the promised ten bob.

Five shillings (25p) each meant that we could afford the bus fare to a favourite pub, the Cambrian, several pints of scrumpy at fourpence (2p) a pint, then fish and chips. First call was at the pub, where we started on that notorious rough cider that is known simply as scrumpy. In its roughest state it looks almost

30

green and requires a dash of lemonade to make it acceptable to the least discriminating palate.

While we were supping scrumpy we got involved in games of cribbage, which would not have mattered if John and I had been bad players. We were not and the prize for winning each game of cribbage was a pint each of scrumpy. We won eight or nine games in a row, so that we drank about thirteen pints of scrumpy, which is enough to get anyone's back teeth awash and we were still under-age anyway. While we were sitting down playing cribbage there were few complications but when we stood up we found that locomotion was definitely a problem.

We had reached that unusual, but fairly widely experienced stage of intoxication, in which it is quite feasible to walk backwards, but not forwards. I cannot explain this phenomenon even now, but I can assure you that it is authentic and that it makes life very difficult for anyone so afflicted.

John Ingram and I backed out of the pub with all the dignity we could muster as crack crib players and manoeuvred our way across the street to the chipper, kept by an Italian named Frank. Though he cannot have been all that used to seeing people who looked as if they were going out of his shop when in fact they were entering, Frank was most accommodating. He served us and while we were waiting was persuaded to entertain us with a ballad, sung in his very pleasant tenor voice.

There was no aggro in those days and we enjoyed our chips, eaten rather unusually while walking backwards as we retreated towards our homes. We negotiated the route remarkably well in the circumstances, until we reached the bus garage, into which we backed quite unintentionally, as if we slept there with the double-deckers.

I managed to back out again, making a three-point turn without undue incident, but John, it seems, fell into the inspection pit. I would not abandon a pal in such straits, but you will understand that I had difficulties of my own at that time and was not at my most observant, so I backed off home without realising the extent of his predicament. I came to grief a bit further on, in a field occupied by sheep, where my father found me. Someone had gone to him and said, 'Ben, I am sure that is your Ray in that field down there.'

'Where's John?' asked Dad as he shepherded me home. 'It's all right, he's following on,' I replied.

We had not been back home very long before the wretched John did follow on, in an indescribable condition. He was covered in black grease from head to foot and still had other problems. My family cleaned him up as best they could, sobered him up a little, lent him one of my suits to wear on his way home and a bag in which to carry his own horrible clothing. He hid that in an attic until he could get it cleaned.

I suppose John, like me, got out of the doghouse eventually, but it taught me that pints of scrumpy are not the best reward for winning games of cribbage.

I had my first holiday apart from the family when I was seventeen and a party of seven of us went off to the Butlins camp at Clacton, where we boozed away most of our time and money in the predictable manner. I did manage to win the camp snooker competition, for which I received a trophy that was particularly modest. Nowadays you can win a holiday prize.

I was still in my teens when during a Blackpool holiday I met a girl called Marion, from Burton-on-Trent. This was the first romance that lasted beyond the summer, for she used to visit me in Tredegar and I would travel by train to see her in Burton. We even got engaged, but the travelling was a bit of a bind, snooker meant too much to me and I was not yet ready to settle down.

By coincidence, some years later I had occasion to go to Burton-on-Trent with a friend, who was making a business trip. As I sat waiting for him in the car I saw Marion on the opposite pavement, pushing a pram. She did not see me and I did not try to attract her attention. We were on the other side of the town from her home, so it really was a chance sighting. I would admit to an odd feeling as that part of my life walked away, though in truth I was not exactly short of engagements in those days and I am not talking about snooker.

I never neglected my snooker practice, though, always play-

ing for an hour and a half or so every night before joining my
mates in the Punch House for a drink. I even played darts for
the Punch House team in those days. Some nights we would go
on from there to the Queen's Ballroom and dance to Herbert
Jones's Orchestra. I always enjoyed dancing and even at the
age of fifteen or sixteen, on my trips to London for the snooker, I
used to go to dances at the famous Hammersmith Palais.

Do not think that all my energy was expended on snooker
and dance halls. I still went swimming regularly and after a
shift in the pit I would either cycle or run up the Dommon to
keep fit and to enjoy the fresh air after being underground.
Right at the top of the Dommon there was a wartime gun
emplacement and I would stand on the parapet and look down
over Ebbw Vale. I was always alone at such times and I
preferred it that way. I still enjoy my own company, but I was
much more of a loner in my teens than I am today. You soon become gregarious when you do the rounds of holiday centres and
exhibitions.

As a teenager, though, I felt on top of the world when I stood
on that summit. Perhaps it was symbolic of my innate desire to
be world champion. I knew that was where I wanted to be, right
at the top.

In the china cabinet at my home in Werrington, on the out-
skirts of Stoke-on-Trent, is a small tray I won for reaching the
Welsh final of a tournament run by the *Sunday People* newspaper. I finished runner-up in Cardiff. I never had any success
in the Welsh boys' championship or the English boys' under-
sixteen event, but I did reach the British under-eighteen final in
1949-50, losing to another Welshman, Jack Carney, of Pontar-
dawe. It was that all-Welsh final in London that brought me to
the notice of the BBC for the first time, though in the event they
did not learn very much about me.

Jack and I were invited to be interviewed by Angus McKie
on radio's *Sports Report* programme. Jack was questioned first,
then I was asked to pinpoint Tredegar, a place that was not
exactly on the tip of people's tongues in the London of those
days and probably is not now. I mentioned the Rhondda and

33

Merthyr Tydfil, then Ebbw Vale, at which point the interviewer said, 'Ah yes, that is where Aneurin Bevan was born.' I
pointed out that Ebbw Vale was Bevan's constituency and that
the Minister of Health in the Attlee government was in fact
born in Tredegar, but my interviewer would have none of that,
whereupon an argument developed and the listeners never did
get to known anything about me as a snooker player.

Perhaps that interview did reveal something about me as a
person, for I have always been prepared to challenge anything
with which I disagree, whether it be in snooker, mining or any
other sphere of life. I like to have a go, but I would not wish anyone to get the impression that I am what the Army scathingly
call 'a barrack room lawyer'. It is just that I like to get things
straight, but when I find I am in the wrong I am willing to go to
considerable lengths to make a personal apology. The fact is
that the BBC man was wrong about Aneurin Bevan.

I will never forget that trip, including the way I lost to Jack
Carney, for I was 12 in front and there were only four balls left.
The brown was quite a tricky shot and what I had to do at all
costs was to miss the pink, which like the black was on the
cushion, for Jack needed three of the last four balls. I used too
much left-hand side in potting the brown and the cue ball flew
up the table and kissed the black, which was dead on the top
cushion. The cue ball hit the side cushion and spun back behind
the black.

I swerved the cue ball round the black and hit the blue, but
knocked it into the jaws of the baulk pocket. Jack knocked in the
blue, rolled the pink down the cushion into the pocket, then potted the black to win the championship. As I said, I had no luck
with the interviewer either.

(*Right*) Police-Constable No. 184 Reardon in 1962

(*Below*) Joe Davis in action at Worcester City Police Club in 1962, where I managed to beat him for the first time

(*Above*) Entertaining friend and rival John Spencer after defeating him in the final of the English amateur championship in 1964. Our host, Jim Westwood, then Lord Mayor of Stoke-on-Trent, stands on the right. (*Below*) In South Africa with Jonathan Barron for the 1967 Test series

4
CENTURY AND TITLE

The real fault is to have faults and not to amend them Confucius

My progress as a snooker player took a big bound forward in 1949, when I was seventeen. John Ford, of Abertillery, was in great form at the time and he went on to become Welsh champion after giving me a 4-0 thrashing that made me realise with startling clarity that I was merely a potter of a snooker ball, while he was the master of the cue ball and of the stun screw shot. Losing to John Ford did not bother me in the least, for I realised that I could learn more from him than from anyone else I had encountered in my career, if what I had done to that point warranted such a description.

It may just have been that I was now more receptive and windows were opening in my mind, but I spent the next month or so in daily practice at the institute, on my own, perfecting the techniques of which I had become aware. Pretty soon I drew my first dividend, a maiden century break of 101. That really made all the effort worthwhile.

I only had to wait another three months to hit the jackpot, for in his first defence of the title John Ford met me in the 1950 final and I beat him 5-3 to take the championship of Wales for the first time. I did not imagine I had learned it all, for a fluke shot had played an important part in my triumph. I missed the pink into the top pocket and it came back off the cushion to roll down into the middle bag. There was no denying my progress though, as the record book shows. I won the Welsh title for six years in a row, the last time being in 1955.

John Ford was my opponent every time, except in the 1953 final when I faced a player named Aubrey Kemp, who like a lot of other people enjoys a drink while he is playing. When he met me in the Welsh final he was determined to take things very seriously indeed, so much so that when someone offered to buy him a pint during the first frame he ignored his parched throat and politely refused.

It did not do him any good, for I was playing well and he soon saw the writing on the wall. After the second frame I heard him say, 'Get me a pint, Dad, I am not going to get anything this time.' He was right, but he did win the Welsh title five years later.

From the start my great rival was the lad from the Lucania in Tredegar, Cliff Wilson, who reached the English boys' final the year after I did and also won it in the following two years. For some reason he always lost to me in the Welsh championship and beat me in the qualifying competition for the English championship, in which Wales was only entitled to one representative. I never got a crack at the English championship until pit closures in South Wales caused our family to move to North Staffordshire in 1956.

I suppose I had quite a lot to do with this move, for I could see things were getting more and more serious and I kept telling my parents that the prospects were bleak. I urged Dad to seek a transfer to another coalfield and he did, but my mother was never very happy about moving to strange surroundings away from the places and the people she loved.

Dad went first on his own and they gave him accommodation at a miners' hostel at Knutton, which is part of Newcastle-under-Lyme, a 'loyal and ancient borough' that adjoins Stoke-on-Trent. This hostel was really a camp with prefabricated huts in which displaced people from the continent had been housed after the end of the war in 1945. Most of them could never go back to their homelands and quite a few of them stayed on to work in the mining industry in North Staffordshire.

There were men of many different nationalities from all over Europe and their traumatic experiences in wartime and subsequent exile made them uneasy and suspicious. Understandably they were slow to take anyone on trust and I think it must have been the result of my father's work in the National Union of Mineworkers that made him an exception. Whatever the reason, when I followed with the rest of the family to North Staffordshire he was already well known and well liked. Dad was employed at Florence Colliery at the southern end of Stoke-on-Trent and I joined him there to find the familiar camaraderie that is part of the unwritten law of the miner. It was a cosmopolitan work-force, with Poles, Italians, Latvians and so on, but first and foremost they were all miners. Perhaps the foreigners worked just a little bit harder than we did, even compulsively, but that too was only to be expected.

The only other difference I noticed was that the work-force as a whole were a little less safety conscious than we tended to be in South Wales. It seemed to me that Welsh miners were more aware of the need for dust suppression and I noticed that miners at Florence would take small, calculated risks by working a little bit ahead of the roofing. Whereas in South Wales we would have sat down and waited until the props were in place, they would press on willingly.

He knows not his own strength who hath not known adversity

Ben Jonson

Let me make it clear that what I have just recalled had nothing to do with the fact that I almost died in that pit on 30 April 1957.

There is no way I would blame anybody, anyway, for Dad was safety officer at Florence Colliery and what happened to me was just an example of the risks of mining coal.

I was helping to enlarge a roadway at the coalface when the top heading caved in and I was trapped for three hours by the rubble, so that I was unable to move a muscle, feet, fingers or face. Ironically, I had expended a fair amount of energy and effort in two attempts to break up the boulder that saved my life. I first had a go at it with my pick and next I tried a pneumatic drill, but the boulder defied me and I decided to leave it so that it could be used by the next shift for packing. If I had managed to break up that boulder . . .

It was while I was kneeling beside the boulder, shovelling coal back behind me towards the conveyor, that I felt a trickle of dirt on my helmet. Instinctively I recognised the tell-tale signs and flung myself forward. Overhead was a 12ft long girder of considerable weight and it crashed down, falling across the boulder instead of killing me. Just to underline how lucky I was to escape, let me tell you that there was a fatal accident of a very similar kind in the same pit two weeks later.

Fortunately for me, the support girder and the boulder caused an open space that just allowed me to breathe, otherwise I would have been asphyxiated by the dirt. They say that the proximity of death helps to concentrate the mind and that must be true, for I realised that what I must do was to lie doggo and not resist. I cannot tell you why I was so sure about this, for I cannot remember ever being given advice on the subject, but I knew that if I struggled against the weight of the rubble my blood pressure might well soar to fatal heights. It was terribly hot and the sweat was running into my eyes. Soon I was numbed from the waist downwards by the pressure.

Twelve men set about the task of removing the four or five yards of rubble under which I was lying. They worked with desperate urgency and I could hear from their initial reaction that they did not think my propects were good. The snag was that as I listened helplessly to the way they were working I knew that they would dislodge the dirt and smother me. Of course they could not see my situation and I could not, at that stage, tell them. It came as a great relief to me when I heard the voice of the under-manager, Jack Winnard, who instructed my rescuers to work from the sides. My only worry now as far as they were concerned was that someone might accidentally catch my fingers with his shovel.

Those three hours before they were able to release me seemed like an eternity. Time that flashes past when you are late for an appointment is divided in these circumstances into individual seconds, limping minutes and crawling hours. To keep myself sane I played in my mind thousands of games of marbles with my little brother, Ron, who is seventeen years younger than me and was only eight at the time. I often used to play marbles with him, so when I closed my eyes it was easy to summon up the familiar scene and play the imaginary games. I was able in this way to stop myself dwelling on my desperate plight and wondering whether the massive girder would slip off the boulder and crush me. It kept me relatively calm and passive.

When the accident happened my father was down another shaft and anyone familiar with coalmines will understand why his dash to the scene left him absolutely exhausted. All he could hear when he arrived was me, sounding like a trapped puppy as I pleaded weakly, 'Give me air, I can't breathe.'

The girder that was poised above me like the Sword of Damocles did not slip. In fact the only mischief it did me was to leave a burn mark on my neck. I was left bruised and sore and I had no other injury. My ordeal had left me looking and feeling a bit like a dirty dishcloth and when the blood started to circulate properly again in my numb legs it had me screaming in pain for a moment or so, but they gave me sips of water and soon I was all right.

In fact, when they got me to the surface and I was taken off by ambulance to hospital for a check-up, the doctors could not believe that all the readings were more or less normal: pulse and heart beat, blood pressure and so on. I suppose it does seem incredible and people find it hard to believe that I never lost a single night's sleep over the accident. I am not being boastful now those terrible hours are years behind me. The fact is that being trapped in that way for so long gave me no nightmares and I am not claustrophobic. I went back to work in the pit quite happily and with no qualms, though when I look back I find myself forced to accept the fact that I must have a fairly tough constitution and temperament.

When I was working in the mining industry I was always ambitious and trying to qualify for jobs with wider responsibilities. In fact I first began to attend evening classes when I was living in Tredegar. At Florence Colliery I became fire officer, then in 1958 attended full time at the North Staffordshire Technical College to take a course.

41

I have a certificate signed by the principal, Dr E. R. Patrick, to show that I first of all satisfied the examiners that I was able to recognise the various gas caps formed in a flame safety-lamp in atmospheres containing one and a quarter per cent by volume of inflammable gas and more; and that my hearing was good enough for me to carry out the duties of a deputy.

In October 1958, Raymond Reardon, of 12 Bath Street, Weston Coyney, Stoke-on-Trent, was granted a shot firer's certificate by the Minister of Power, on the recommendation of the Mining Qualifications Board and in pursuance of the Coal Mines (Explosives) Regulations, 1956.

Two months later, on 2 December 1958, the Minister of Power granted me a deputy's certificate, this time on the recommendation of the Mining Qualifications Board in pursuance of the Coal and Other Mines (Managers and Officials) Regulations, 1956.

Around this time my intelligence quotient (IQ) was assessed as being in the MENSA class, which is flattering if it is true, even though I have no intention of putting it to the test.

Anyway, it was obviously felt that I was reasonably bright, for I was one of three people who were offered the opportunity to take a degree course at Ruskin College, Oxford, as trade union members. I was grateful for the offer, even though I turned it down. Somehow I do not think the academic life is for me.

My caution as a shot firer was not always popular, for I always stuck strictly to the book of rules and fired one shot at a time. Some of the men who had production and bonuses on their minds would say when they found I had been allocated to them, 'We've got the Slowboat to China again.' This was a reference to a popular song of earlier years and it was not intended as a compliment to my shot firing.

A wise man turns chance into good fortune   Thomas Fuller

My escape from death was typical of my good fortune in 1957, a year that got off to a marvellous start as far as I was concerned.

Through horse racing, snooker king Joe Davis had become friendly with a Stoke-on-Trent sportsman named Billy Carter, who used his influence to persuade the great man to play me at the Ash Bank Country Club, near my present home. The match was on 19 January, and Mr Carter's twenty-one year old niece, Sue, was helping to sell tickets. That night led to my getting a wife and my famous old cue.

I must have made a fairly good impression on Joe Davis, for he invited me to appear with him eleven days later in his snooker series on BBC television's *Sportsview* programme. Each player invited was given five minutes in which to make a break and I managed 21. It turned out to be the best break of the series and a highly rewarding one for me, since it landed Joe's prize, which was a hand-built cue. That cue became almost as much a part of me as my right arm.

Sue knew nothing about snooker when she met me, but that situation did not last long. When fellow players held an archway of cues over us as we walked from nearby Bucknall Church after our wedding on Easter Monday, 1959, it symbolised the major role the game was to play in our lives.

Sue worked in the pottery industry as a freehand painter for Messrs Johnson Brothers in Hanley. It took me some time to get used to the idea of having not only a wife but a working wife, for in South Wales at that time most of the married women stayed at home and baked the bread. Sue was one of the women who form a large part of the work-force in the pottery industry. Soon she had an additional job as my unofficial secretary-manager and keeper of records.

Lots of people have assumed that the accident at Florence Colliery put me off working in the pits and they are wrong, but Sue was not happy about my working underground and in any case as a married man it was my duty to think rather seriously about the future, certainly more seriously than I had done in the past. At that time Stoke-on-Trent had its own police force and I knew that the Chief Constable, W. E. Watson, encouraged his officers to take part in sport in their off-duty hours, so I applied to join and was accepted.

I enjoyed most of my training for the police force, with the exception of the five mile runs on which we were sent from the Mill Meece centre. I was a smoker and I liked a drink. Moreover, I did not bother much with exercise after working in the pit, so I was out of condition as far as running was concerned and very soon I was left trailing. I did not try very hard and at times I would stop and chat to people working in their front gardens.

Sergeant Blyth used to be waiting for me at the Mill Meece gates when I arrived, a good half hour or so after the previous man. The glowering and reprimands did not bother me. I used to say, 'I am not built for speed, I am built to last.'

My seven years and eight months in the force that is now amalgamated with the Staffordshire County Constabulary were mostly spent pounding the beat in the Hanley Division. As a probationary constable in 1960 I got the princely sum of about £12 a week and after five years of police service my pay went up to about £20 a week. I was lucky enough to get two commendations from the recorder at the Stoke-on-Trent Quarter Sessions.

To get the first one, Police-Constable No 184 Reardon arrested a burglar. I was on duty in Hanley one night when I spotted an open window on the top storey above a chemist's shop. I radioed for assistance, then followed the route I guessed the intruder had taken, which involved shinning up a drainpipe and getting in through the window. It did not cross my mind that I was at my most vulnerable while making that particular manoeuvre, but all was well, for I found my man crouching under a table and probably cursing his luck. By the time reinforcements arrived I had him handcuffed and waiting.

I was even luckier on the second occasion, when I was informed via my personal radio that a man with a shotgun was coming to Hanley to deal with a married man who had treated his unsuspecting daughter rather badly. Though I was given the name of the armed man, it did not ring a bell until in a crowded shopping arcade in the middle of Hanley I saw the familiar face of a man I had known when I was a miner and I remembered that he had that surname.

44

I was able to approach him as a friend and it was immediately apparent to me that this was the man about whom I had been warned and that he was indeed armed and also hopping mad. Fortunately he listened to reason and in the end gave me the loaded gun and walked with me quietly to the police headquarters. If the officer attempting the arrest had been a stranger I do not know what might have happened, but it was a lucky break for me and an even luckier one for him and the man he was seeking.

I have a certificate signed by the Recorder, Kenneth Mynett, QC, and the Chief Constable, W. E. Watson, stating that 'Constable (184) Raymond Reardon has been commended by the Recorder of Stoke-on-Trent for his commendable action which resulted in the arrest of a man for being in possession of a firearm with intent to endanger life.' It is dated 27 May 1963.

First the pit accident; then this man with a loaded gun; then when I announced that I was going to leave the police force and take up snooker full time I was told not to be so foolish, that such a course would be far too hazardous. Years later the then Chief Superintendent, Frank Shepherd, recalled his worst ever advice when he appeared on television in the *This is Your Life* programme in which I was featured.

My move to the Potteries was lucky in all sorts of ways. When I first arrived there I knew nothing about the area, so that in my free time I scouted round for one or two snooker halls and won a shilling or so, but what I really needed was a headquarters to take the place of the institute in Tredegar, where I could get in some serious practice. An overman at Florence Colliery, Fred Gray, was a member of the Rowley Moody Liberal Club in Hanley and he introduced me there. Nobody ever asked me how I voted.

It was a fairly modest club, right in the centre of Hanley, which was very convenient. Among the members were some businessmen who became good friends and supporters. The accent was on snooker and there was no licensed bar, which was just as well, for I have never been too keen on having drink in the playing area, though in touring round the clubs in this

45

country it is something I have learned to tolerate.

Mind you, I have always enjoyed a drink after a game and so after one of my early visits to the Liberal Club I went out of the door, turned right and went into the Market Tavern a few yards higher up Percy Street. There was a dartboard in the bar and I put my name down for a game.

I did not know a soul in the place, but soon I was called to make up a foursome. Typically of the Potteries, in no time at all I found I was among friends. One of the darts players was Huston Spratt, picture editor of the local evening newspaper the *Staffordshire Evening Sentinel,* and another was Bernard Phillips, who worked at Ashworth's pottery off Broad Street, Hanley. They helped me to settle down very quickly and soon I knew almost as many people as I did at home.

Both those chance acquaintances are still good friends. When Sue and I married a couple of years or so later, Bernard Phillips paid for the wedding cars and he still turns up when I play in championship matches. Huston Spratt and Hanley Liberal Club combined to provide the wedding album we still treasure. Can you wonder that I took a liking to the Potteries?

I made a break of 128 in practice at the Liberal Club before my first match for them in January 1956. It was in the Rose Bowl competition of the North Staffordshire Orme Billiards and Snooker League and I was to win many of their trophies.

In my first year at the Liberal Club I made breaks of 142, 109 and 132 in successive frames when playing against Jack Window. Harold Phillips, the Billiards Association and Control Council chairman, sent a certificate to the club to commemorate the feat.

Now that I had moved from South Wales to the Potteries I found I had more scope to qualify for the English amateur championships final and two days later I was at the Burroughes and Watts Hall in London, with a tough job on my hands. My opponent was Tommy Gordon, who had already won the national amateur crown twice, in 1949 and again in 1953. He started a clear favourite to complete his hat-trick in 1956, though some of his supporters must have experienced doubts when I surged

7-3 ahead in the final, which involved twenty-one frames over two days.

Now there came one of those moments of misfortune that can turn optimism into despair. It was one more lesson to be learned by me, but it would not have been the classroom and the time of my choice. Just as I was sailing merrily along, the tip came off my cue and there was no way in which I could effect an immediate repair. It had always been my practice to use adhesive wafers to secure the tip on the cue, but after this wretched experience I switched to Araldite. Now we saw an early example of just how much a familiar cue meant to me, for using a substitute I lost five frames in a row and went on to lose to Tommy Gordon by 11-9. I still do not like to hear any sportsman talking about a sticky patch!

My best friend is the man who in wishing me well wishes it for my sake Aristotle

One of the happier aspects of that trip to London was my renewed friendship with one of snooker's real characters, a one-armed newspaper seller, who believe it or not was named George Orwell. He had a business based upon a canvas bag that was wrapped round a lamp post near the tube station at the corner of Oxford Street and Soho Street. I first met him when I travelled to London from Tredegar for the boys' championships.

George was a snooker fanatic and despite the fact that he had only one arm he could play well enough to get through the London qualifying rounds. Once I went to play a few frames with him in a billiards hall in Oxford Street and I noted that when the ball was near the cushion he could cope with it as well as anybody I had seen, finding his disability no problem. We played seven or eight games and I remember he had a break of 66.

He always seemed to be around the snooker scene in London and appeared to know everyone and everything. I suppose he first spoke to me when I was walking along the pavement carrying my cue in its case. He would know the boys' championships were taking place and would guess that I was going there. He asked me who I was and where I came from and luckily he took a shine to me. Thereafter, if he spotted me walking towards him, he would invite me to dive into his canvas bag and sample the crackers and cheese he kept there with the newspapers. Then he would ask me about the tournament, tell me about my most formidable rivals and advise me in many other ways.

In the days when I first met George Orwell I found the plush setting of the Burroughes and Watts Hall a bit intimidating and by my standards at that time the table was ultra-fast. George noticed I was having difficulty in potting balls into the middle pocket and he soon spotted the reason why. I was playing shots off the pink spot into the middle pockets too slowly, so he told me to play my natural stun shots.

He also pointed out that the thick nap on the table could lead to the pace varying from day to day. Instead of aiming for the angle of the pocket and trusting to the nap to pull the ball in, George told me to aim at the widest part. I took his advice and found that as usual he was right, for it solved my problems.

Apart from the mishap with the tip of the cue, that defeat by Tommy Gordon also underlined the fact that my safety play was too limited, for I was tending to leave the ball somewhere near the baulk cushion, without making absolutely sure that it rolled into a position that would give my opponent the maximum amount of trouble. When I analysed my play I also realised that I lacked what is usually called killer instinct, which is not to be confused with dark thoughts of homicide. What was happening was that when I had made a break of 30, 40 or even 50, I would let my concentration wander and miss a shot, letting my opponent back into the game. Not for the first time I took careful stock of my techniques and set about the business of improving them.

I met Joe Davis a number of times and he was kind enough to describe me as a future British champion, but unknown to both of us there were some lean years ahead.

It is not enough to aim, you must hit   Italian Proverb

I was looking forward eagerly to the 1957 English championships, for I was playing well and fancied my chances. In March,
during practice, I had my highest break to date, 139. Just before
that I had compiled a break of 128 and things were looking
good, especially when I reached the semifinals, but I played
badly at the wrong time and lost to Stan Haslam, of Bolton,
who was the beaten finalist that year.

Hanley Liberal Club sponsored my entry in 1958, but again
my form deserted me at the crucial time. In practice at the club
I made a break of 131, but in London I lost in the semifinals to
Marcus Owen. It was little consolation to me that I beat Stan
Haslam, my conqueror of the previous year, when he visited
Stoke-on-Trent and played me in the more relaxed atmosphere
of the Ash Bank Country Club.

Perhaps it was that I had my wedding on my mind in 1959,
but whatever the explanation I went to London to make my
fourth attempt to win the amateur title and lost 5-2 in the first
round to Trevor Scott. It was very disappointing, to say the
least. I had to take a frank look at the situation and discover
what it was that was going wrong. I came to the conclusion that
the remedy was the drastic one of dropping out of the
championships for a year or two in order to stabilise my game,
working on the long pots and on ways of taking charge of the
situation.

It did not mean going short of competition, for there were
many events in which I could enter. In the autumn of that year
I reached the Club and Institute Union national semifinals,
losing in Doncaster to T. Graham of Spennymoor.

There were plenty of requests for charity matches and exhibition games, some of them with a Stoke-on-Trent friend, David
Deakes, who won the British boys' billiards championship in
1955, beating G. Waite, of Treorchy in the final. David had
been runner-up the previous year. He and I are currently plan-
ning to open a very handsome snooker club in Hanley, with
facilities that reflect the remarkable way the game has moved

49

up-market in the past decade.

Jack Window, who was one of my friends at the Liberal Club in Hanley, used to run me around to matches and exhibitions in his Ford Prefect, an old banger of a car. I called it the Gutless Wonder and in motion it did sound a bit like a badly-maintained washing machine, but it still got us to where we wanted to go and home again, carrying us something like 6,000 miles. Eventually Jack sold the Gutless Wonder to me and this was my first car. In my early days as a professional I had to sell it and I made a profit of £30. The man who bought the Gutless Wonder did not do too badly, either, since he managed to sell it for £35, though he did have a half-shaft go shortly after becoming the owner.

I went one step further in the Club and Institute Union competition in 1960, beating London jeweller George Humphreys in the semifinals, then went on to lose in the final in Doncaster to Doug Roberts, of Middlesbrough. This was the year in which I decided to join the police force.

5
SERGEANT'S PERKS

Policemen are soldiers who act alone   Herbert Spencer

Two years later, in 1962, I won the Great Britain police snooker championship for the first time, beating another Welshman, Constable Brian Jones of Pengam, in the final. This was the occasion when, after I had won the first two frames with the aid of half-century breaks, an inspector named Chandler from Shropshire asked me in all sincerity, 'Do you do any beat duties?' Our Chief Constable was a pretty keen sportsman, but unfortunately for me he did not place the same emphasis as the inspector did on snooker achievements.

When I was not doing beat duty on foot I was riding round my area on a heavy duty bicycle that would have given a Milk Race competitor a recurring nightmare. Policemen had not taken to patrolling in cars to such a degree at that stage and the neighbourhood bobby had a value that is now being appreciated once more. It has its snags of course, because the boundary between on-duty and off-duty tends to get obliterated as people come to you with their problems, but in my view the bobby who knows his patch is of vital importance.

I remember an occasion during one winter when I was cycling in the Abbey Hulton area of Stoke-on-Trent just after the pubs had shut in the afternoon and a snowball fight developed between adults on a scale that was a nuisance to residents. There were too many people involved for one policeman to deal with alone, so I used my radio to summon assistance, realising only too well that it was an egg-on-the-face situation.

I looked around and spotted one undersized man I recognised. He was the one, I decided, not because he was one of the smaller combatants, but because my background knowledge enabled me to place him near the root of the trouble.

I grabbed him and it was all over, for when the police cars arrived from all directions, very impressively, the salvos of snowballs had ceased and the rivals were drifting away. Obviously, I had guessed right. We whipped the trouble maker back to the station and kept him for a while, but you cannot really describe snowball fights seriously in court, so we let him go with a warning.

My career in the police force got off to an odd start as I set off on my beat in Hanley early one morning, on duty in uniform for the first time. Near the bottom of Hope Sreet I saw a man sweeping and washing down the pavement outside a butcher's shop and despite the helmet he recognised me. 'Is that you, Ray?' asked Dennis, who managed the butchery business and was also head waiter at the Ash Bank Country Club. I had known him some years, so he invited me in for a cup of tea.

Off came the cape and helmet and I had just taken my first sip of the tea when the door opened and in came my sergeant, Dick Twiss, a huge man who was the Staffordshire police heavyweight boxing champion. He was too experienced to show much surprise and he just said, 'Didn't take you long to find this tea call, Ray.' I got up to go, but Sergeant Twiss said, 'Finish your tea and I will see you back at the station.'

When he had gone, Dennis asked, 'Will you get into trouble?' I thought it was quite possible, so Dennis told me to let him know what happened. When I asked why, he said, 'Never mind.' When I went back to the station for a meal break I reported to Sergeant Twiss, as instructed. He asked me how long I had known Dennis and when I told him he sent me away with a general caution about how I should carry out my duties. I rang Dennis to let him know that I was all right and it was then that I learned why the sergeant was annoyed. He had been getting the food for his breakfast from Dennis for years, then taking it back to the station and cooking it there. A big man like him needed good food.

I soon realised that Sergeant Twiss was keeping a special eye

(*Above*) Playing against Fred Davis in the quarter-finals of the world professional championship of 1969/70. (*Below*) Nothing could surpass the excitement of winning the world professional title for the first time in 1970

(*Above*) My first big cheque. The 1970 world championship. (*Below*) With Perrie Mans, the South African snooker champion, in 1973

on me after I had stumbled upon his perks. This made me wary, especially on occasions like the snowy night when I decided not to patrol part of my beat on one circuit, but to take a short cut along the canal towpath.

I had not gone far when I came upon a drunken man who declared his intention of jumping into the canal. I advised him to think again, pointing out that the water would be freezing cold. In any case, I told him, I was not going to jump into the water to rescue him because I could not swim. That was not true, of course, but I would not fancy swimming in that canal at any time and certainly not in the early hours in the middle of winter.

When the drunk persisted in saying that he would jump in, I guessed that he was only after sympathy and did not really intend to do so. I said to him, 'Look, give me a couple of minutes to walk off that way, then if you want to jump into the canal, get on with it and remember it will be freezing cold.' I walked off. As soon as I got round the corner I peeped back to see if my guesswork had been right. It was and he took himself off home.

I went off again along the towpath on my short cut to the Eagle Pottery, where I knew I could get a cup of tea. Sergeant Twiss was also aware of this fact and I was wary, for when I got near the pottery works I walked backwards to the door, so that the one set of footprints in the snow looked as if they had been made by someone leaving the premises. All I had to do was to bang on the door and identify myself to the watchman, who quickly let me in out of the cold. I had only just arrived when I heard a vehicle brake outside and guessed it was Sergeant Twiss in the divisional van.

The watchman and I kept out of sight with our cups of tea while the sergeant banged on the door and shone his torch. I said to the watchman, 'Don't answer him, just tell him when you next meet that you must have been at the other end of the factory.' I heard Sergeant Twiss say to Alfie Botfield, the driver: 'We have missed him. Look at those footprints. He has gone.' I finished my tea and sneaked out by another door to get back on my beat and make my way to my next check point. Parked near it was the divisional van.

'Good morning, Sarge,' I said. 'We missed you at the pot-bank didn't we?' he replied. I said, 'I don't know what you mean, Sarge,' and he drove off, leaving me well aware that I had to watch my step, backward and forward.

From a police point of view my snooker career was still thriving. Towards the end of 1962 I managed to beat Joe Davis for the first time. We were at Worcester City Police Club, where Joe was giving four blacks start to all-comers. When I stepped forward, Joe said, 'Mr Marker, cut that lead to 21. I have played this young man before.' He had beaten the other three policemen he had played that night, but after he had broken the frame against me I made a break of 96 and beat him 125-20. I was mighty proud to have beaten a man who won the world title twenty times, even if it was not in championship conditions. Sergeant Taff Evans, who had organised the affair, was at least as proud as I was that night.

My top achievement of 1963 was to retain my Great Britain police title at the Pontin's camp in Blackpool by beating Sergeant Kellow, from Glasgow, 2-0 in a semifinal and Constable Agnew, of Cambridge, 3-0 in the final.

My form was good enough to persuade me that I should tackle the English championship again. I had been out of the competition for four years and in the previous one, 1963, the championship had been divided into two sections, with the top player from each meeting in the national final.

When the English amateur snooker championship Southern Area heats began on 17 February 1964, at Burroughes and Watts Hall in Soho Square, London, R. Reardon of Wolverhampton, if one is to believe the official programme, had a bye in the first. At this stage all the matches were over seven frames and in the second round I beat D. G. Thorneycroft of Cornwall, 4-1. My third round opponent was another Cornishman I. J. James, who lost 4-2.

In round four I gave Cornwall a respite, beating A. Barnett of Wednesbury, 4-0, which took me to the semifinals ten days later at the same venue against yet another Cornishman, this time Jonathan Barron, the antique dealer from Mevagissey, who became the television champion. In the fourth round Jonathan had beaten Gary Owen, the first world amateur champion of the previous year, 4-0.

I had a century break in beating Jonathan Barron 5-3, which earned me a place in the final against J. T. Goodwin of Birmingham, whom I beat 6-2 to take the southern title. That success over Halesowen salesman Jack Goodwin brought me face to face with the Northern Area's top man, John Spencer, a twenty-seven year old cost clerk from Radcliffe in Lancashire. At that time he was virtually unknown in snooker, though he very quickly put that right.

John was destined to become world professional champion in 1969, a year before I did. He took the title off me at the end of 1970 and won it again seven years later, meanwhile finishing runner-up in 1972 to Alex Higgins.

John and I have met many times since that 1964 amateur final, but we have never encountered championship conditions more ludicrous than those we found in Birmingham's Central Hall, where an attempt to enforce a non-smoking ban nearly caused John to walk out at the start. Spring was at its brightest and best and the afternoon sun shone straight into our eyes through the huge, uncluttered windows. Even the reflection from the watch on my wrist dazzled me.

It was five-all at the end of the first day's play and I had a 74-break in winning the last two frames of the second afternoon session to lead 8-7. John won the first frame of the evening session to level the scores once more, but that was the last success he enjoyed. I went on to win the next three frames and the coveted title with an 11-8 victory for which I had been trying since my teens. It was eight years since my first appearance in the final and I was thirty-one years of age. John Spencer, incidentally, lost to Pat Houlihan in the 1965 amateur final and finally landed the crown the following year, when he beat Marcus Owen.

My one great sadness is that my mother did not live to see me win the English title, for she literally sacrificed her happiness to make it possible. She died in the year before I was finally successful. Mother never really settled after leaving Tredegar and she pined for the familiar places, but she was totally unselfish and would never put her own interests before those of her family.

When Billy Carter, Sue's uncle, first introduced me to the world of dinner jackets, black bow ties and white silk scarfs, mother went into debt to make sure I looked the part.

After losing his wife Cynthia, my father was helped by Sue's mother, Florence Carter, who was a widow. They became so fond of each other that marriage was in the air, then Ben was hit by another blow. Sue's mother died on his birthday.

I suppose it proves that the Reardons and Carters get on very well together, but I wonder what they would have made of my paternal grandmother, who smoked a clay pipe and did not speak a word of English!

By now Sue and I had moved from my father's house at 12 Bath Street, Weston Coyney, Stoke-on-Trent, to a police house near my present home. The new address was 8 Birchgate Grove, Bucknall, but I was not there all that often. When I was not on duty as a policeman I was travelling up and down the country playing matches with John Spencer, Gary Owen and others. In November 1964, I was seen on ITV playing against Gary at the City Transport Club, Leeds.

Every calamity is a spur   Emerson

There was a shock awaiting me when I went to the Burroughes and Watts Hall in January the following year. The programme had restored me to Stoke and I began with a 4-1 win against S. Hyams, of the Home Counties. In the second round I won by the same margin against M. V. Eldridge, of Portsmouth, then I did it again by beating Jonathan Barron 4-1 in the third round. My semifinal opponent was G. Thompson, of London, and I notched a comfortable 5-1 victory to qualify to meet thirty-five year old Deptford barrow boy Pat Houlihan in the final.

I was in all conquering form, or so it seemed, needing only one of the last five frames to make sure of retaining my southern title. Then I was 61-43 ahead in the last frame, lost it and crashed out of the championships. Imagine it! I was 5-1 ahead and lost 6-5. The Londoner's smash and grab raid on my title left me dumbfounded, but I reckon one shot was the turning point. With the score at 5-4 I had a chance in the next frame to take the brown and the other ball I needed to win.

What happened was that I played the brown slowly, intending that the cue ball should bounce off the side cushion and stay on the blue. It was a wrong shot, because if I missed the brown I was sure to leave it sitting in the jaws of the pocket. Pat knocked in the last four balls to win the frame and level the scores. Then he won a black ball decider.

I could have played the brown firmly with left-hand side, to miss the middle pocket and leave the blue in the baulk pocket, or I could have played a slightly more risky shot, which I would prefer. That would be to pot the brown with some screw and left-hand side to swing round on to the blue off three cushions.

It was a bad mistake and one I have never repeated. You remember your mistakes in snooker and after some years there are not many shots or positions that are new to you.

Pat Houlihan, as I have said, went on to beat John Spencer in the national final.

For me it was pick-yourself-up-again time and at least a success in July made me feel a bit better. I met another Welshman, Terry Parsons, the Welsh champion from the Rhondda, and beat him in the Club and Institute Union competition final in Coventry. Terry won the Welsh championship again four years later, though the most significant thing about my win over him in Coventry was that it meant I had won, in the space of twenty years, every senior trophy for which I had entered.

My son, Darren, was born in November 1965, so that it was not a bad year. But I was unhappy about losing the title so soon.

The following year the national title eluded me again. I beat Birmingham's Graham Miles in the Southern Area semifinals, then lost in the final to Marcus Owen, brother of Gary, who beat me 6-4. Northern champion John Spencer beat Marcus 11-5 in the national final.

Once more I found some consolation when I won the Great Britain police title for the fourth time in five years, beating Sergeant Melbourne, of Manchester 3-0 in the best of five frames at Birmingham Police Sports Club over two days. The police tournament was a big affair, attracting some 800 entries from all over Britain.

My adopted city of Stoke-on-Trent did me proud in April of 1966. My father went with me to Stoke Town Hall, where the Lord Mayor Alderman J. A. Boon, received me in his parlour and presented to me a civic plaque and paid me some nice compliments. More Stoke-on-Trent presentations lay ahead.

Gradually snooker was becoming more ambitious. A week long tournament staged by the Coventry Works League proved that the game had drawing power, for the attendances were splendid. I did not help much, being eliminated at an early stage, but Gary Owen and John Spencer produced a great final, which Gary won. These two were going to Karachi for the world amateur snooker championship and a number of players, myself included, took part in matches to raise money to finance their trip. There was not much available in the way of grants.

There was a rather sad occasion at the end of March 1967, in the closure of the famous Burroughes and Watts Hall in London's Soho Square. It had stood for 130 years and had been a stage for all the giants of the game. On the final night I was one of the players who took part in a testimonial to Richard Holt, editor of the *Billiards and Snooker* magazine. It seemed strange that this great hall should go at a time when interest in the game was beginning to boom.

I beat R. W. Jackson of Shepperton, 4-1 in the Southern Area first round and he managed only 25 points in the last three frames after making a break of 43 in winning the second. My second round opponent was G. Jackson of High Wycombe, who had the worst possible start. He gave four away and I followed with a break of 96 (13 reds, 11 blacks, 1 pink). I won the frame 112-20 and the second 90-19, but my opponent then fought back and restricted me to 66-49, 46-43. This was encouraging, but my form again proved to be erratic when I lost 4-2 to

Jonathan Barron in the third round. He lost to Marcus Owen, the holder, in the Southern Area final.

I went to Belfast for an exhibition match to raise money for the Newspaper Press Fund in Romano's Ballroom in Queen Street and had a 3-2 win against world amateur champion Gary Owen, then I went off on my first tour abroad.

He that hath a head of wax must not walk in the sun
                                                English Proverb

On the invitation of the Transvaal Billiards Control Association, Jonathan Barron and I went to South Africa for six weeks, including a Test series. The United Tobacco Company, contributed £500 to finance the tour and Potteries demolition contractor Ron Colclough lent me a safari suit.

Our Test opponents were Mannie Francisco, the South African champion and a Cape Town sales representative, and Jimmy van Rensburg, formerly of Natal, but now of Zimbabwe, who had won the title seven times and had been beaten in the most recent final by Mannie Francisco. For the other matches, eight players were chosen from each of the three provinces, Natal, Cape and Transvaal.

Our first match on 1 June was with Transvaal in the Ken Shaw match room in Johannesburg, where we won 4-0. I beat Arthur Heyes 4-1 and Ray Morley 4-1. We went on to beat Northern Transvaal by the same margin at Berea Park, Pretoria, where I beat Ernie Antony 4-0 and Lou Rademeyer 4-1.

We flew to Durban and had a couple of free days before beating Natal 4-0 in the Municipals Club. I beat Ronnie Hollis 4-1 and Franz van Wyk 4-0. We flew to Port Elizabeth to meet the Eastern Province in the Athenaeum Club, with a slightly different format. I beat J. van Niekerk 2-0 and Jonathan beat R. McIver 2-0 in the singles, then we beat C. Woods and J. Harmse 2-0 and W. Billson and L. Gerber 2-0 in the doubles. On the second day Jonathan beat Van Niekerk 2-0 and I lost 2-1 to McIver, but we won both doubles 2-0, against Billson and Woods, and Gerbert and Harmse.

61

We met Western Province in Nick's Billiards Club and dropped our first match. I beat Sylvano Francisco 4-3 (he beat Jonathan by the same margin) and Rodney Siderfin 4-0.

Then we flew to Cape Town for the first Test at Claremont Civic Centre, where it was my turn to lose. Jonathan beat Francisco 4-0 and Van Rensburg 4-1. I beat Francisco 4-0, then lost 4-2 to Van Rensburg. We flew back to Durban for the second Test at the Municipals Club, where we really flopped, losing 4-0. Van Rensburg repeated his margin over me and Francisco also beat me 4-2. My excuse was that I had sunstroke. Jonathan lost 4-1 to Mannie and 4-3 to Jimmy van Rensburg, but I cannot remember what excuse he made.

The third Test was in Johannesburg in the Ken Shaw match room and we won 4-0 to clinch the series 2-1. This time I beat Van Rensburg 4-1 and Francisco by the same margin. Jonathan won 4-2 against Francisco and 4-1 against Van Rensburg.

During this trip we had a breathtaking view from the top of Table Mountain, which is 3,567ft high. It seemed a long way from the Dommon as I looked down on the hundreds of ships that were forced to make the journey round the Cape in these days shortly after the Suez calamity.

Another memorable day of sightseeing was a visit to the Kruger National Game Reserve, where the total silence made me feel that time had stood still, that life had stopped and no one would ever age.

It was in Johannesburg that I first met Perrie Mans, the South African who has given up trying to convince the media his real name is Pierre. I made four century breaks during this tour, including one against Perrie when I beat him 9-2 in an exhibition game of seventeen frames.

It was quite an honour to be selected for this series, since neither of us was the national champion. It was three years since I had won the English amateur title and Jonathan was three years off his first win in that national final. Harold A. Phillips, chairman of the English Billiards Association and Control Board, saw us as ambassadors to South Africa and he went to the trouble of getting special permission from the Stoke-on-Trent Watch Committee for me to make the trip, since I was a serving police officer. Ken Shaw, managing director of Union Billiards, and Eric Lichfield, sports editor of the *Johannesburg Sunday Times*, were also influential figures in the success of our tour.

We drew packed houses of 500 to 600 everywhere we went and in six weeks the game had more publicity than it got in six years in this country. There were even radio commentaries and our experience as a whole convinced us that the game would go over big in Britain, with the right venues and publicity.

It was a strenuous tour, socially as well, with parties almost every night. Jonathan Barron is a taciturn man to say the least of it, so I had to do most of the socialising, which I enjoyed. Perhaps that is why Ken Shaw promised to arrange another tour of South Africa, if I would turn professional. It was an offer that made me think.

At that time there were only ten professionals, including one of the pioneers, Joyce Gardner, compared with eighty or so now. These were established men like John Pulman, Fred Davis, Kingsley Kennerley, Rex Williams and Jackie Rea, who had recently been joined by John Spencer and Gary Owen. There were not many tournaments and even fewer sponsors, so the professional ranks almost amounted to a closed shop to which newcomers were not exactly welcomed with open arms. New professionals were accepted, but then it was made pretty clear to them that it was a case of every man for himself.

Turning professional was very much on my mind when I returned home from South Africa in July and had the very pleasant task of presenting to my brother Ron a Castella Player of the Month award for making a break of 118 at the Mackwith club in Neath. Ron achieved this feat when he was only sixteen and I did not get my first century break until I was seventeen.

If you look in the Billiards and Snooker Control Council handbook you will see that in 1966, R. Reardon (Stoke) lost to J. Terry (Ystradglynais) in the final of the British boys' snooker championship. Do not be puzzled: that was my brother Ron.

6
TAKING THE PLUNGE AS A PROFESSIONAL

In the day of prosperity adversity is forgotten Apocrypha

When John Spencer took the plunge, he was the first new professional since Jackie Rea, sixteen years earlier in 1951. John had fewer prospects in his career than I had and above all he was unmarried and had just had a difference of opinion with the Control Council. Gary Owen followed suit, for he had twice won the world amateur championship and felt he had little more to accomplish in their ranks. He was part-time at first, remaining a Birmingham fireman and keeping engagements when off duty. It would not be feasible now.

I decided to become a professional as from 3 December 1967, leaving the police force at the age of thirty-five. Riley Burwat, the table equipment firm, gave John Spencer, Gary Owen and me small retainers, which helped a bit, but it was very tough going.

One of my first moves was to write to the National Spastics Society, offering to stage exhibitions on their behalf. I received an answer saying they were very interested, had looked at my career and would like to talk to me. The interview was arranged at a Leeds hotel and since I had not got a car I sought the help of my friend Huston Spratt. He had just bought his first car, an Anglia, and I drove it to Leeds, full of hope. We found the hotel and the meeting place. There were two officers of the Spastics Society, one of whom had travelled from Scarborough and the other from the London area.

We talked, then they said in effect, 'Carry on being a policeman and we will tell you when we can find you some work.' I replied that I intended to be a professional with or without work from them and we drove back to the Potteries with some uncharitable thoughts. If that was all they had to offer, why had they gone to the expense of travelling to Leeds and why had they dragged us the 200 miles to and from Stoke-on-Trent? One or two of my friends said, 'If that is the way they waste money they will get no more from me.' They meant it too.

From the start I was determined not to accept jobs that paid only a fiver. The offer had to be around £25 or so and the standards had to be reasonably good. I wanted the professional snooker player to be worthy of respect and to be properly rewarded. Nowadays, that £25 has grown to something like £450, plus VAT. No one could have forecast in 1967 that by 1981 Steve Davis's manager would be negotiating fees in excess of £1,000 for a personal appearance of the champion.

I was glad to work on a casual basis in the publishing room of the *Staffordshire Evening Sentinel* in Stoke-on-Trent and as a painter and decorator to keep my head above water in the first twelve months. Perhaps I should have stayed in the police force and tried hard for promotion. At least the £351 I got from them as a rebate on my superannuation payments helped to keep the Reardon family eating regularly, but every household bill posed a problem in those days.

I played a charity match for the National Spastics Society in Kent, but fittingly my first private professional engagement was on 28 March 1968, at Hanley Liberal Club and the Davis family were involved. I beat Fred Davis 7-2.

Inevitably the early days of my professional career were to land me in some odd situations. One of my earliest dates was at Hambridge Mills, Somerset, and when I arrived there I began to think I had been hoaxed. I had to climb a fire escape to the first floor clubroom and when I got there I could see about forty people and a bar, but no snooker table. It was no leg-pull. A ladder was pulled down from a trapdoor in the ceiling and in the room above there was a perfectly good snooker table, even if the headroom was restricted for a six-footer like me.

They were nice people and I enjoyed my visit, but I had not

up to that time come across such an odd place to keep a snooker table. Much more recently I encountered a similar situation at a private house in Kilmarnock, where steps were pulled down to give access to a table in the attic space. Again the headroom was limited and my fear was that my skull might be among the breaks that were made.

Politics is a strife of interests masquerading as a contest of principles Ambrose Bierce

My promised return visit to South Africa came when I needed it most. I was sponsored by the Johannesburg Tobacco Company and Union Billiards Ltd. Fortunately my form was spot on. I made century breaks at the Modderfontein Club: a 120 against Hans van Zyl and a 125 against Transvaal skipper Ken O'Kennedy. The next few weeks yielded three more: 102, 117 and 100, in fact I got 16 in six weeks, the best being a break of 136 in the Orange Free State.

My best effort on the tour was a 142, five short of a maximum, and I was pleased to equal Horace Lindrum's record of 26 century breaks in four and a half months. It took my total of century breaks to 324, a figure for which I can vouch, for I used to keep meticulous records. In recent times I have become less efficient in this respect, for the total is well over 3,000 now. Anyway, in the course of this second visit to South Africa I travelled 11,000 miles and everywhere I went I was overwhelmed by hospitality.

There is no way I can ignore the question of my trips to South Africa, even though I suppose that it is tantamount to a do-it-yourself entry on the blacklist. I cannot dodge the issue and I have made some very good friends in that country. My tours there were tremendously important to me in my early years. I did not go there as a politician, but simply as a player trying to earn a living and to become established in the sport of my choice. The only world I was trying to change was the world of snooker.

I have many memories of my visits to South Africa, including the journeys I made alone, driving a car through hundreds of miles of a country where there were few English speaking people and where a breakdown might have had disastrous consequences. At that time I just did not appreciate fully the risks I was taking, for I was still relatively new to world travel.

There were some games of snooker that were played under very strange circumstances. There was one occasion when I wished my exhibition game was not such a big attraction, for in addition to the spectators we were plagued by insects, which were attracted by the bright lights that shone down on the table. We had to stop at the end of every frame so that the insects for whom the attraction had proved fatal could be brushed from the table. In between, the bodies that littered the green baize were an additional hazard.

On another occasion I played at a spick and span venue that had a different kind of snag. The floor was so highly polished that I could not keep my feet. This was at a colliery club near Johannesburg and there were about sixty people watching, so I stuck it as long as I could before pointing out that I could not do myself justice in these conditions. Officials were very apologetic and asked us all to go into the bar while they dealt with the problem. My guess is that there was quite a panic and probably some hard words were said about the person who had tried hard to ensure a polished show. The solution, though, was unbelievable, for when I got back I found the floor had been covered with scouring powder of the Ajax type, commonly used in most kitchens. You can imagine the state we all got into trampling on that surface and I shudder to think what it did to the floor.

There are times when well intentioned and enthusiastic officials are guilty of the most amazing errors of judgement. When I reached one club in England I could not believe my eyes when I was shown the table. A club official told me proudly that because it was not in pristine condition he had taken off the cloth and had dry-cleaned it at a nearby launderette. He seemed aware that it was a rather unusual colour when compared with other snooker tables, but he had no idea what he had done to

67

the nap. It was a nightmare to play on, but he had meant well and we managed to complete an exhibition that seemed to please the customers.

An ashtray made from a lion's paw stands in the lounge of my home to remind me of another wacky occasion when I was in South Africa. I was invited to spend the weekend playing snooker on a farm at Senekal in the Orange Free State and I accepted, even though it meant a drive of 200 miles from Johannesburg. When I reached the town to which I had been directed I was somewhat taken aback, for it looked exactly like a scene from a familiar Wild West movie, with only one main street and one hotel. I found a telephone in the hotel and even managed to cope with the lady operator, who spoke only Afrikaans, so that I was put through to my intended host, a farmer named Jurie Human. He said to me, 'Stay where you are, don't move,' which tickled my sense of humour, for where I would move to from that hotel I could not imagine.

He drove over to collect me and I followed him back over twenty-five miles of dusty roads to a huge farm, where I identified the bungalow in which the family lived, several sheds and other buildings which I thought might house the snooker table and also some round huts with grass tops, called rondavels.

My host was a huge man, standing about 6ft 7in tall, with hands like shovels. I tend to lay a fair amount of store on a firm handshake, but he could make a power press wince. He and his family are lovely people and they made me feel instantly welcome. In the bungalow I was offered a cup of tea I really needed, then as usual I was anxious to check out the job in hand. 'Where is it?' 'No, not the loo, the table.' To my amazement I was taken to one of the round houses, which was about 12ft in diameter. Inside they had placed a full sized snooker table, with each of the four corners touching the wall. If you had taken the roof off and looked down, you would have been gazing at a plan of a square peg in a round hole.

They had engaged me for the weekend, to entertain the family with some of my best tricks and shots, yet I had to crawl under the table when I needed to take a shot from the other side or either end. I have heard of snooker handicaps, but this was ridiculous. I think of it whenever I catch sight of that ashtray in my lounge, for it was made from the paw of a huge lion shot by my host. The taxidermist did a better job than I was able to do that weekend.

Driving to and from Johannesburg took me through some delightful scenery, but on my own I found it a boring business, with roads dead straight for eighty miles or so at a time.

Fuel economy is an important subject in South Africa, so petrol was always a bit of a problem on such trips, since filling stations closed from noon on Saturday for the rest of the weekend. I had 400 miles to cover from Phalabora to Durban and there is also a 50mph speed limit, which in the event I feel I may have fractured slightly. I filled the petrol tank on the Friday night and asked for a call at 4.30 am, an hour with which my times in the pits and the police force had made me regrettably familiar. I managed only a light breakfast before leaving half an hour later. By 9 am I was in Carolina and in case anyone thinks I was going faster than Concorde let me state that this one is in the Transvaal. I drove straight on to Ladysmith, the town in Northern Natal that is remembered for the long siege it withstood under Sir George White in the South African War at the end of the last century. I filled up again at Ladysmith and the time was 11.57 am, so I had three minutes to spare before the petrol pumps were closed. I was only fifty miles from Durban now, so I was OK for the weekend. That is how you have to plan your journeys, like a military commander making sure of his supplies.

For the latter part of my stay in South Africa in 1968 I had the company of my wife Sue, and Darren. Sue was expecting Melanie, our daughter, but she was able to stay with me over the Christmas period, which was great for us all.

We shall sooner have the fowl by hatching the egg than by smashing it Abraham Lincoln

My visit to South Africa put me in good heart for my first tilt at the world professional snooker title. The game's growing prestige was illustrated by the award in the New Year Honours List of the MBE to Gary Owen.

John Player sponsored the world championship and there was £3,500 in prize-money. By comparison Steve Davis picked up £20,000 for winning the same championship in 1981. In 1969, in addition to myself there was John Pulman, the defending champion, plus Rex Williams, Fred Davis, Gary Owen, John Spencer, Bernard Bennett and Jackie Rea. It was arranged to play the quarter-finals in Bolton, Stratford, Southampton and Stoke-on-Trent.

My baptism came in the British Legion Club in Tunstall, the most northerly of my adopted Five Towns of Arnold Bennett fame. There on 20 January I began a five day battle with Fred Davis, who had been boys' billiards champion as far back as 1929 and had more than 1,000 snooker century breaks to his credit. He beat me 25-24 and taught me new dimensions of the game.

Twenty years earlier a defeat by John Ford was the catalyst in an improvement that took me to the Welsh amateur title. This defeat by Fred Davis was even more important, for I absorbed more in that one match with him than I had learned in all the intervening years. A defeat before my home crowd would normally upset me a little, but on this occasion it was well worthwhile for the sake of the tactical experience I gained. Over the five days a total of 1,500 people saw some of the tightest snooker ever played. There were some bleary-eyed people around the Potteries, for the afternoon sessions went on from 2.30 to around 7.30 at night and there were times when I feared the evening sessions might go on all the way to breakfast time. It was like teaching a young colt not only to respond to the reins, but to use them to restrain himself.

I was three ahead with six frames to play, but Fred's safety play enabled him to retrieve the position. I won the first frame 58-20 and lost the next two, 69-8, 66-7. I had a break of 43 in levelling at 2-2 by winning the fourth 77-22 and was 47-12 ahead in the fifth before Fred cleared the table with a 67 break. I

(*Above*) A visit to Florence Colliery with father Ben Reardon in 1973.
(*Below*) Demonstrating the 'bottle shot' on my trip to India in 1974

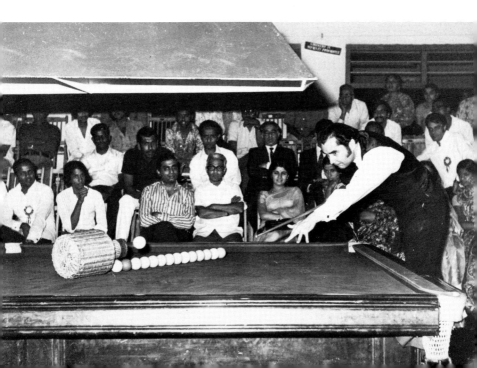

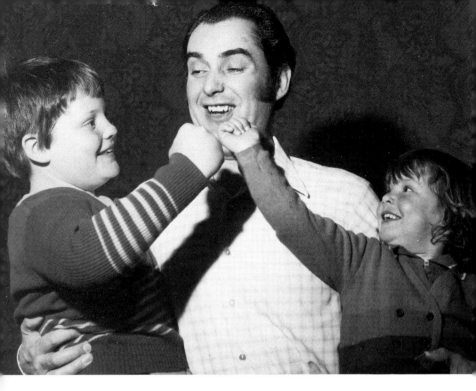

(*Above*) Our dad's a knock-out! Darren and Melanie help me to celebrate winning the 1974 world championship. (*Below*) Running for a helicopter with Eddie Charlton on our 1974 tour of Australia. During the flight a door flew open at 1,000 feet up

had a 44 break in levelling again with an 80-17 win and took the lead with an 80-33 win to lead 4-3 overnight.

When the second session began I won 94-36, but Fred took the next two by 60-9 and 76-24 to draw level. The best break of the match, an 89, was the only score in the eleventh frame and I also won the next 84-38 to restore my two-frame lead. Fred replied with wins of 68-29 and 68-52 to finish the second day all square. The next session went (my score first): 70-39, 19-97, 60-65, 86-16, 102-19, 77-41, 7-74, so I was one ahead. I had the best break of 56 in the fifth frame.

Next day the marathon sessions continued: 54-39, 36-50, 71-59, 37-63, 71-43, 79-18, 60-71. In the evening it went: 26-62, 23-60, 21-62, 22-63, 36-50, 106-31, 14-84. I had gone from two in front to three behind, but in the afternoon of the last day I won 64-27, 70-24, 70-54, 68-34, 56-48 to go in front by two frames. Fred won the next 74-42 and I took the next 71-1 in a frame that had lasted thirty-five minutes before a ball was potted. I started the evening session with a 72-50 win to go three ahead. The session had not started until 8.30 to give us a little respite.

Fred responded with two wins, 63-28, then 58-21 in a frame that took seventy minutes. Next he won 57-29 to level and went ahead with a 64-32. I drew level by winning 92-27 and he pipped me by taking the last frame 68-4, having fluked the first red, missed an easy yellow and struck the pack with the cue ball without leaving me a red. It was all tension and concentration and I like to think that I pushed Fred a bit that time.

These were the days when I forged another link that was to prove invaluable to my career as a professional snooker player and it came about through a city councillor in Stoke-on-Trent, Cyril Finney, who knew I was having a struggle. He put me in touch with Pontins, who engage sporting stars to entertain their holiday-makers. I was interviewed and they took me on, even though I was not a champion. That is why I have always remained loyal to them, for thirteen years now.

The Pontins circuit, as it has become known, involved from the start driving almost 1,000 miles a week. I would drive to Lowestoft on the east coast, on down to Rye on the south coast and along as far as Weymouth, covering ten camps in five days, giving exhibitions, doing trick shots and holding clinics. All the camp managers were most hospitable, none more so than Don Green at Breen Sands, Somerset, 6ft 4in tall and once a bodyguard to Prince Charles; Willie and Doreen Jorgensen, at Sand Bay, Weston-super-Mare; and Jim Butler, at Broadreeds.

It was through Derek Hardy, then manager at the Dolphin camp, Brixham, and now South West manager, that I opened up that area in 1973. Now I drive 230 miles down to Torquay on a Sunday night for twenty weeks from May to October, visiting six Devon and Somerset camps each week. It is a lovely circuit and I have been friends for years with Derek Hardy and his wife, Helen, Jim Fields and his wife, Marjorie, and all the others. Pontins have always been loyal to me as I have to them. It is a wonderful job, we have a great understanding and it is all very dear to me. It was through Pontins that I started to play golf, at the Churston course when I was at Brixham. There I met the secretary, David Webb, and bank official Mike Gilbert, my best mate. We play golf regularly in the summer and I stay with Mike and his wife Maureen, on occasions.

I suppose I do not need the circuit now, for there are plenty of exhibitions and big fees, but I remember the time when the income from this source kept me afloat. In any case, I still love doing the circuit. I have made many friends at the centres and the holiday-makers have always been great, thousands and thousands of them.

Meeting so many people, whether at holiday centres or elsewhere, clearly poses problems, for you are always seeing faces that are vaguely familiar and the name and identity have gone. One such predicament afflicted me at the Bracklesham Bay centre in 1973. When I got there I tracked down the entertainments officer to tell him of my arrival and he mentioned that a new referee would be on duty. I asked who the newcomer was and grumbled a bit when the entertainments officer could not tell me, since it is always better to greet people by name, especially if it is someone you ought to know.

Sure enough I knew the face. It was very familiar, but I could not place the referee at all. He said, 'You don't know me, do you?' When I asked who he was he replied, 'Never mind, it will come to you.'

As soon as I could I got round to the entertainment officer's office and we carried out a search of the records. At last we identified the referee, as my cousin! It was Dan Reardon and I had not seen him for twenty years. I nipped back quickly, but he had left. I was most embarrassed and when I told my family, some laughed at the story and others tut-tutted and said, 'Fancy you not recognising him.'

I made up for it when Dan Reardon next came to a camp to referee my matches, but the extra fuss on that occasion did not make up for the red faced business of our first encounter.

This incident is one of the reasons I always tell people my name when I meet them. Quite often they say, 'I know very well who you are,' but I do not mind that. It is a worthwhile practice to save embarrassment, especially on the odd occasion when even a really well known face leaves a blank in your mind where the name should be. There is no harm in saying, 'Hello, I am Kevin Keegan . . .' always providing you are, of course. On behalf of those who like me are not equipped with a photographic memory, can I appeal for this policy to be adopted?

Public men are bees working in a glass hive
Henry Ward Beecher

Problems of being recognised by people I could not identify increased tremendously after the introduction of the BBC-2 *Pot Black* series on television. Suddenly we had to get used to being recognised wherever we went, being greeted as a friend in the streets of every strange town.

Television producer Philip Lewis has been quoted as saying that the idea of the series came to him as he lay in bed pondering ways of increasing the impact of colour television. Eight programmes of fifteen minutes each were recorded in a Birmingham studio that had been a cinema. Finding people to watch one-frame snooker was a major problem and on occasion canteen staff were drafted in to make up the audience. More than 1,200 people can now be accommodated in the Pebble Mill studio, but the demand for tickets comes from all over Britain and before one series is completed there is a waiting list for tickets for the following year.

Four cameras were used and the main one was in the studio gantry some 25ft above the table. This meant that the customary shade over the table had to go and at first there were some qualms about the players being affected, but they were groundless.

The series was completed within four days in the early summer of 1969 and the outcome had to be kept secret until it was seen by the viewers in instalments almost a year later. The programme went out at 8.50 pm and coincided with the news on BBC-1, but it was an instant success, with the help of 'the whispering voice' of commentator Ted Lowe.

I beat John Spencer 88-29 in that first final and also had the top break of 99. Winning the gold-plated Pot Black Trophy was a landmark in my career. Yet I had quite an argument before I was allowed to take it out of the studio. It is a distinctive trophy, incorporating a television aerial, but the BBC are not too keen on letting it out of their custody.

There is such a small margin between top class players that I was never very keen on the formula for Pot Black. I reckoned you could hold four such competitions in successive weeks and get four different winners, but it is difficult to see any alternative in the face of so many other commitments and there is absolutely no doubt about the tremendous impact on the public.

What I did not know when I won that first Pot Black series was that the real breakthrough lay just ahead.

7
FIRST OF SIX WORLD TITLES

He who aspires to be a hero must drink brandy   Samuel Johnson

At the end of 1969, from 15 to 20 December, I had my second world championship battle with Fred Davis. The draw for the quarter-finals was: John Spencer v Jackie Rea; Fred Davis v Ray Reardon; Gary Owen v Rex Williams; John Pulman v David Taylor. Though the championships had the backing of Player's No 6, the success of the quarter-finals was dependent upon the number of tickets that could be sold and the attendance the previous year gave me a 'home' match again.

This time the arena for our war of attrition was Longport Workingmen's Club, Stoke-on-Trent, where I was 5-2 ahead at the end of the first session, with a best break of 47 in the fourth frame. (Scores were (mine first): 75-47, 68-38, 38-91, 76-20, 66-51, 65-44, 26-59.) We were level at 7-7 at the end of the evening session, during which I had a break of 62 in the ninth frame and Fred had one of 63 in the eleventh. (The scores went: 37-79, 80-29, 64-26. 42-93, 4-59, 17-65, 50-60.)

The next day I won the first six frames in the opening session, (56-28, 65-21, 48-45, 69-61, 90-12, 56-19). I had breaks of 48, 47 and 43. The first of these came in the seventeenth frame in which Fred was leading 45-0. I won it on the black. In the next frame I was trailing 61-22 and came up with a 47 to win. Fred had a break of 56 in winning the final frame of the session 70-11, leaving me 13-8 ahead.

In the evening session this became 16-12. Fred had a break of 78 in the sixth frame of the session and I had a 45 in the next. (Scores: 41-97, 66-46, 40-71, 50-59, 22-86, 75-6.)

Play the next day was slow and cautious. Fred played safety shots as only Fred can and he also had breaks of 63 and 51 in winning the first two frames, 25-102, 4-90. We shared the next two, 63-40, 50-61, and each was a prolonged battle in its own right. I had breaks of 41 and 42 in winning the next, 84-28, then had a 41, but Fred compiled a 58 and won the frame 45-80. I made a 45 break in the last of the session and won it 74-52, to lead 19-16.

In the afternoon session of the fourth day I took six out of seven to stretch my lead to 25-17. I had breaks of 61 in the third frame, 118, a championship best, in the fourth, and 51 in the fifth. (The scores went: 63-50, 91-6, 61-71, 118-13, 88-42, 61-50, 105-19.) Fred was not about to surrender and he made it 26-23 by winning six of the seven frames in a three and a half hour evening session, combining safety play with breaks of 47, 53, 57. (Scores: 1-72, 79-7, 39-86, 27-78, 30-89, 13-72, 16-77.)

Fred started off with a 58 break in the afternoon session the next day in taking the first two frames 34-78, 26-49, cutting my lead to 26-25. I regained the lost ground with wins of 74-1 and 93-36, the second one including a break of 59. Fred won the next 73-52 with the help of a break of 42 and I took the last 88-2, including a break of 62.

That made it 29-26 and I was in luck in the next frame, especially with a blue that went in-off the pink, which I cut in to win 64-53. That was really the clincher, for I took the next two 93-19, 67-34 to take a winning lead of 31-26.

I played better than in our previous meeting and was amazed at how Fred could stop you from seeing any of the reds when they were all on the table, but there is something else I remember about this encounter.

The fact is that I had to battle with flu as well as with Fred Davis. At the end of the fourth day I realised I was playing well and feeling awful, so something had to be done. Once more I gambled and it gave me victory over the second of the famous Davis brothers. Instead of going home to bed at the end of the very late evening session, I stayed at the club drinking champagne cognac, an expensive kind of medicine you cannot have prescribed on the National Health Service. I took an overdose, too, but it was Fred who got the hangover. This very acceptable medicine did the trick, I felt fine when I went to the snooker table for the next session and even my form sparkled. I played vintage stuff.

I got £175 for the first round win and was sure of another £250 even if I had lost the seventy-three-frame semifinal against John Spencer at Bolton Co-op Hall from 16-21 February. It was our first competitive meeting since the English amateur final in Birmingham in 1964.

I went ahead 4-2 and 8-5, making a break of 58 in the third frame. (Scores (mine first): 24-69, 66-30, 87-39, 39-67, 74-18, 75-56, 57-36, 25-65, 74-30, 49-30, 67-41, 41-77, 57-59.) I had a break of 71 in the nineteenth frame and was 14-6 ahead (after scores of: 59-30, 36-73, 55-54, 66-43, 76-31, 83-20, 113-22). Then I slipped back to 15-11, even though I took the twenty-third frame on the black up. (The scores went: 9-58, 26-47, 65-58, 40-62, 14-83, 48-86.)

Some of the problems we were encountering in turn were psychological, for at times we were both erratic, but the table was far too tight for a championship. You could not pot the black off the spot at speed with much confidence. The ball was drifting and skidding everywhere and side was uncontrollable. We went to 18-14, and 21-18. (The scores: 61-10, 79-54, 50-25, 11-76, 45-54, 1-120, 1-71, 52-44, 29-74, 78-34, 52-68, 40-68, 68-24.)

I had a 5-1 session, including an unfinished break of 69 to stretch my lead to 26-19. (Scores: 61-31, 68-27, 83-10, 69-65, 132-0, 45-67.) John closed the gap to two in the next session. (The scores were: 16-79, 25-75, 46-43, 40-82, 65-41, 62-23, 60-9.)

Two wins in the next session gave me a winning lead of 32-26. The remaining frame scores were: 58-10, 27-67, 5-58, 53-51, 14-54, 49-75. With the game over I got a break of 93, the best of the week, in one of the remaining frames.

Crowds were tremendous, so that the dour and somewhat mediocre play was a great pity. Most of the blame could be placed on the condition of the table, even though it was the same for both players.

My opponent in the seventy-three-frame final at the Victoria Hall, London, from 6-11 April, was John Pulman, of Bromley, who had qualified by beating two former world amateur champions, Dave Taylor and Gary Owen, beating the latter 48-25 in Middlesbrough. John Pulman had held the world title from 1964 until John Spencer took it off him in 1969. By reaching the final we had made sure of receiving £475 and there was £750 more for the winner and £500 for the loser. Rewards were beginning to come, though, of course, the amounts were chicken feed compared with today.

Just when I thought I was going to be a runaway winner in the final, I had a real shock. For the first four days my long pots were going into the top pockets like bullets and John Pulman was struggling. I took the first frame 82-42, with the aid of a break of 63, then won 57-40 to make it 2-0. (The scores went: 14-68, 72-12, 78-40, 31-70, 66-26, 61-60, 78-48, 53-64, 69-44, 16-118, 59-32, 1-102, 37-80, 81-22, 73-56, 89-47, 59-72, 79-65, 65-58, 52-71, 8-92, 26-95.)

I was now 14-10 ahead and I ran into form. I had breaks of 33 and 57 in winning the next frame 114-9 and a 73 in taking the next one 73-24, then a 46 in winning 78-47. Then it went: 56-36, 40-90, 31-72, 77-45, 55-81, 54-29, 7-44, 7-116, 115-19. In the last frame I had a break of 93 and was 22-14 in front. I won the next five, 85-23, 68-38, 53-52, 62-38, 69-27 to make it 27-14.

It was beginning to look good for me, but John finished the session with a win by 81-32, then the evening session went: 56-63 (on black), 62-47, 49-69, 87-36, 39-70, 8-118. I was leading 29-19 and I really lost my concentration, perhaps because it was only the second seventy-three-frame match in which I had ever played. I lost 2-70, 44-70, 46-64, 9-64, and was only 29-24 ahead. I made a break of 85 to clear the table and take the next one 104-33, halting the slide, but as a reporter said, to come from 13 behind and win would be the greatest recovery since Lazarus and John did not seem to think that was an exaggeration.

He won 33-86, 24-81, then I replied with 73-7, 90-15. John took the last two 19-75, 38-99, and was four down with 13 to play.

On the Saturday I won 83-0, then lost 45-57. Then it went: 67-17, 17-100, 41-64, 30-100, 31-69, so the score was 34-33. It looked as if I had blown it, for John was ahead in the frame that would have levelled the scores, when there came one of those dramatic moments that make snooker such a tense spectacle and can send hopes plummeting like a lead bucket down a well.

John played a safety shot that was just not quite safe enough and I managed to produce the sort of shot I needed if I was to survive. I squeezed one red past another into the top pocket and rolled the cue ball up behind the green. I made a break of 38 to clinch the frame 68-30 and it restored my confidence and ended John's magnificent fight back. I had a 40-break in winning the next frame and took the following one 49-23 to take a winning lead of 37-33.

I was Stoke-on-Trent's first world champion in any sport. My best break in the final was a 94, but the critical one was that break of 38.

Nothing will ever surpass the wonder of winning the world crown for the first time and the moment of victory is imprinted indelibly on my mind. Now I knew that the gamble had succeeded, that I could settle my debts and that the lean years were over. They had been well worthwhile.

One of my earliest encounters as champion was with the new comet that had appeared in the snooker skies, Ireland's Alex Higgins. The Belfast player astounded everyone by winning the Northern Ireland and all-Ireland championships early in 1968 when he was nineteen, and three months later he became the youngest professional in European snooker. He was soon reinstated as an amateur, but launched himself properly in the paid ranks a year or so later.

My first meeting with him was at Burscough, near Liverpool, where I quickly realised that here was a rather wild lad with a touch of genius and a great capacity for attracting crowds of spectators and also the wrong kind of publicity.

Alex was being advertised as the man who made a break of 136 in six minutes. I did not see it or time it, so that the only comment I will make is that he is an excitingly fast potter and publicity was good for his cause when he was trying to make a name for himself in the early stages. Against me Alex made a break of 78 and a voice announced, 'Three minutes twenty-four seconds.' I went to the table, potted a red, stood up, looked around and said, 'One red, one second.' That went down well with the crowd and I went on to win the match, but I had plenty of respect for Alex and still have, for he is a tremendous player when on song. In 1972 he beat John Spencer to become the youngest ever holder of the world championship.

The trouble with Alex is that he tries to cram a week into every day. He lives, plays, smokes, drinks and functions generally as if it were his last chance. It worries his friends to see him squander his nervous energy and a lot of his opportunities, for shooting stars arc a spectacular course, then burn out.

There is no well-defined boundary between honesty and dishonesty
O. Henry

South Africa and Australia were on my schedule for the autumn of 1970 and I ran into near disaster. On 20 September in South Africa I played an exhibition match at the Atlas Aircraft Company's Recreation Club and afterwards put my cue down on the table in order to free my hands to sign autographs. I felt the cue go and thought someone was putting it back into its case for me, but suddenly, when the last autograph had been signed, I realised to my horror that the cue had gone.

When club officials realised what had happened they acted quickly. The police were called, no one else was allowed to leave the premises and cars were searched, but there was no trace of my precious cue. It is difficult to describe to anyone the anguish and torment I suffered. This is the cue I got from the Joe Davis competition and it was part of me. Without it there would be no point in my fulfilling my next engagement, which was to go to Australia and put my world title on the line.

I was desperately afraid that all the uproar over the theft of my cue would cause the person responsible to panic and break it up 'and burn the evidence. Otherwise the cue was easily identified, for it had a brass ferrule and in South Africa at that time they used fibre ferrules, the brass ones being unavailable.

The *Rand Daily Mail* issued an appeal for the return of the cue and in the early hours of the next day someone responded anonymously. He or she left the cue on the steps of the newspaper office with a note attached, written in quite a good hand. It said: 'Until I saw the appeal I did not realise how much the cue means to you. I thought that you probably gave away the cue you used each time, as a souvenir. Please accept my apologies for the suffering I have caused you.'

The story made the front page, an eminent position rarely achieved by snooker. I could not believe my luck in getting the cue back again unharmed and I could not find words to express the relief I felt. I was able to show it, though, for I celebrated the return of the cue with a break of 132.

That break sent me off to Australia in the right frame of mind, for I could not have defended my world championship with a strange cue. Normally, of course, a champion reigns for a full year, but I thought the deal I was eventually able to make in Australia was too good to refuse, so I put it up for grabs in October-November, only six months after winning it by beating John Pulman.

The championships were the first staged in Australia and they were sanctioned by the London based Billiards Association and Control Council, the world governing body. The event was staged as part of the fund raising for a new sports medicine clinic at Lewisham Hospital. The fund was launched by a large donation from the Australian government. It was felt that staging the championships in Australia would increase snooker's standing as an international sport and give greater equality of opportunity to overseas players.

In order to play in Australia I had to miss the Pot Black tournament, in which David Taylor replaced me, and also the Park Drive £2,000 event early in 1971.

The format for the Australian championships was that four players in each of two groups would play each other on a round robin basis, with the top two going into the semifinals.

In Brisbane I beat Patrick Morgan, former Irish amateur champion, who was professional at a top Sydney club, then went on to beat the three other big names in my group, Perrie Mans 22-15; Eddie Charlton 21-16; John Spencer 21-16. The other two semifinalists were both Australian, Eddie Charlton and Warren Simpson. In this tournament I had not played Simpson and John Spencer had not played Charlton and that is how the semifinals should have looked. Instead the two Australians played one another and I met John Spencer for the second time. It seemed to me that a switch had been made in order to ensure that an Australian got into the final. I wanted to debate the matter on television, but there were no takers.

My mistake was that I allowed my annoyance to upset my form and though I had a break of 108, my concentration was not as good as it should have been and John Spencer led 9-3 at the end of the first day of our semifinal. John was in front throughout, leading 2-0, 2-1, 4-2, 6-2. I got progressively worse and trailed 19-5 at the end of the second day, 26-10 at the end of the third and lost 34-15. I must not take anything away from John Spencer, but I did not like the way things were organised, to say the least of the matter.

Eddie Charlton started favourite against Simpson in the other semifinal, having beaten his compatriot many times, but Simpson won 27-22. The forty-eight year old Aussie gave John Spencer quite a fight in the final, before the Englishman won 42-31 to take the £2,333 first prize.

It was some consolation to me for losing my title that from November to January I had the company in South Africa of my wife, Sue, son Darren and daughter Melanie, who was born on 11 May 1969. My finances had improved to the point at which I could buy my first house for the family at 2 Weldon Avenue, Weston Coyney, in the same area of Stoke-on-Trent in which my father lived. I had never liked the idea of taking out a mortgage and I was glad to be able to buy the house outright, with the help of a short term bank loan. Only nine years before, when I was living at 12 Bath Street, Weston Coyney, I had 4s 5d in my Post Office Savings Bank book, which is 22p in the present currency.

Now we had more security as a family and with it came more recognition. Sue and my father Ben, were with me in April 1971, when Stoke-on-Trent paid me a further honour to mark my winning the world championship. The Lord Mayor, Mrs Mary Bourne, presented to me a special plaque.

I had just returned from a tour of Scotland with John Spencer. I beat him 5-4, 5-4, 5-2, 6-3, and lost to him 5-4 in exhibition matches. Neither of us had a century break. The following week I had three in three nights: 101 (all the colours and ten reds) at Aberdeen Conservative Club: 115 in Falkirk and 100 at the Leopold Institute, Slough.

There was always a full book of engagements and the special kind of pressures involved in maintaining peak form. All the travelling and living out of suitcases make it very difficult. I have always been careful not to sell anyone short and even before an exhibition match I like to put in an hour or two of practice. When you get your game right like that, you know you will do yourself justice and so you are confident.

Some of us were playing three or four times a week now, wherever a promoter could be found to stage an event of the right standard. I won the world title four years in a row, 1973-76, after I had learned to live with the pressures to which I have referred. In recent years Terry Griffiths and Cliff Thorburn have found out how tough it can be when you are champion.

In the summer of 1971 on the Pontins holiday camp circuit I was averaging two century breaks a week, that is one in every nine frames. I got a 139 at Bracklesham and a 128 at Camber.

Viewers of Yorkshire Television saw me beat Rex Williams 182-173 in the Park Drive £600 tournament's semifinals, then beat John Spencer 4-0 in the final, in which I compiled a break of 127, the highest ever made on a television programme at that date.

85

I had missed the first Park Drive £2,000 tournament, but I was able to take my place in the 1971 event, starting in October, since Gary Owen had gone to live in Australia. I began with a series of three defeats, the first by 4-3 to John Spencer on 4 October, at Abbey Hey Working Men's Club (WMC), Manchester. (The scores were (mine first): 8-113, 37-75, 106-8, 36-72, 87-23, 98-21, 34-88.) Two days later he beat me 4-2 at Aldwarke Road WMC, Rotherham. (37-93, 6-96, 77-37, 65-53, 31-57, 16-99.) In this match the lights fused when I was in the middle of a break in the fifth frame. There was a lengthy delay and when we resumed I missed and lost. In between, Rex Williams beat me 4-1 at Wyke Non-Political Club, Bradford. (11-67, 44-60, 40-59, 65-62, 61-72.)

On 12 October matters took a turn for the better. I beat John Pulman 4-1 at Balby Ashmount WMC, Doncaster. (74-48, 78-37, 75-44, 37-69, 67-66.)

John Spencer beat me 4-2 at Bateson Street WMC, Leeds. (32-90, 72-67, 66-22, 4-86, 43-66, 0-136.) Shortly before the tournament the top three inches snapped off my cue and though they were replaced my form was being affected. I still managed to beat John Pulman 4-2 at Church Warsop Miners' Welfare. (90-28, 51-71, 42-72, 76-39, 123-7, 80-35.) In the fifth frame I cleared the table with a break of 123. At Wolverhampton Electric Sports and Social Club I beat Rex Williams 4-1. (96-26, 72-38, 77-35, 47-57, 112-1.) I beat John Pulman 4-2 at Pelsall Labour Club. (85-11, 57-65, 63-86, 72-43, 113-7, 70-47.) Rex Williams beat me 4-2 at Wilmslow British Legion Club. (37-72, 42-71, 48-69, 67-23, 89-14, 57-64.)

I finished second in the competition table to John Spencer, whom I met in the final at the RAFA Club, Sale, where I won 4-3. (42-62, 42-74, 69-40, 28-76, 95-16, 98-16, 69-66.) I was a bit unlucky in the early stages, especially when the referee ruled I had moved the blue slightly while potting the green and he gave a foul shot. It all depended on the final frame and John Spencer was 40 ahead. I needed a snooker with only one red remaining and did not get one until there were only two balls left. It gave me first prize of £750, In this final I had my first problems with television lights, for they made the Formica topped Starline cushion rails red hot. They curled and burned my fingers when I played a shot.

We had engagements all over the country. In the Plaza Ballroom, Glasgow, in a match promoted by the police, John Spencer and I played the final frame after the dancing had started. Apparently we had overrun our time. The next two nights we were in Morecambe and the following two in Hyde.

In January, 1972, I met Alex Higgins shortly before he became the youngest ever world professional snooker champion. It was a challenge match in the City Hall, Sheffield, which boasted such refinements as plush seats, carpeted floors, air conditioning and humidity control. Alex was sporting two black eyes and he beat me!

8
TELEVISION PROBLEMS

Doing what is right is no guarantee against misfortune
William McFee

I was matched with Rex Williams and rashly agreed to play our forty-nine-frame world championship quarter-final in Scotland, where we sold the event to various venues. Rex beat me 4-3 at Stonehaven University on 8 November and 5-2 at Aberdeen Conservative Club, where I won 5-2 the following night. I won 4-3 at Glasgow University to level the match and 4-3 at Gourock Torpedo Factory, but Rex went 22-20 ahead by winning 5-2 in Ardrossan.

On the final night at Dundee Masonic Club, I took the first three frames to lead 23-22, but Rex fought back to take the next three and win 25-23. The problem for both of us was in adjusting to the various tables. Rex seemed to do better when the pockets were tight and most of the tables seemed to affect my long potting. I joked that some pockets were so easy you had to be careful not to fall into them while walking past and others were as tight as a mouse's ear.

I could hardly wait for another tilt at the world championship crown. Ladbroke's recognised the major impact snooker was having through Pot Black by making a book on the championship and the magazine *Snooker Scene* assessed my form this way: 'Former pit pony and police horse. Good at controlling traffic. Out of form for a time, which a visit to the cuesmith seemed to put right. Usually shows to better advantage when front running, but a class horse, especially at the generous odds of 10-1.'

The Park Drive sponsored world championship was staged

(*Above*) Joe Davis presents the trophy in the 1974 world championship.
(*Below*) Ireland's Alex Higgins was my opponent in the 1976 world
championship final, held at Wythenshawe Forum

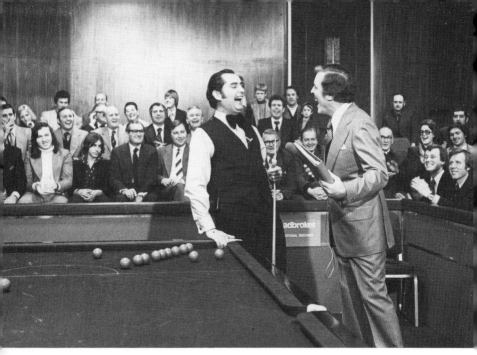

(*Above*) 'Ray Reardon, This is Your Life'. Eamonn Andrews springs the surprise at a recording session in London in 1976. *Thames Television*. (*Below*) Testing John Spencer's new moustache at the 1977 world championship quarter-finals in Sheffield. After holding the title for four successive years I had to accept defeat, and John went on to take the trophy

in the City Exhibition Hall in Manchester in the April. First I had to beat Bacup's Jim Meadowcroft in one of the smaller rooms over a cafeteria and there was so much noise that it was like playing in the middle of a railway station. Obviously snooker players can have their concentration affected by sudden loud noises, but within reasonable limits background noise can be tolerated. On this occasion the volume was greater than anything I had ever encountered in an important match.

The next stage was a bit easier, with only four tables in use, but there were only two people watching when I beat Gary Owen 16-6. I think the lack of an audience bothered Gary more than it did me, for I managed an 8-0 whitewash in the second session.

There was plenty of evidence of the drawing power of Alex Higgins when the semifinals were played. Both matches were staged in the same arena and most of the spectators flocked to watch the one in which Eddie Charlton beat Alex Higgins 23-9. Until that match was finished I felt as if I was playing in a vacuum and it looked as if my hopes were very shaky when I fell 18-12 behind John Spencer. The bookmakers obviously thought I had blown it, for at that stage they would accept 66-1 against my taking the title. I managed to pull one back to make it 19-14, then got to 19-16 when John missed an easy black. However, it was not until the Charlton v Higgins match was over and we had a crowd of spectators that the adrenalin really began to flow.

In all I extended my winning run to seven frames in succession and with the help of a break of 88 in the first frame of the evening session I drew level at 19-19. It was still a seesaw match, but I managed to take the final frame 79-7 to win the semifinal 23-22. Predictably I experienced reaction the next day to the considerable tension of that battle with John Spencer, so that Eddie Charlton thrashed me 7-0 in the opening afternoon session of the final. I pulled myself together and became the first finalist ever to pull back seven frames in the championship. In fact I won the next three sessions, 5-2, 5-3, 7-1 to lead by 17-13, but Eddie Charlton is nothing if not a fighter.

91

Though perhaps he does not possess the range of shots at the command of other top players, he is consistent and can keep a game so tight that his opponent is nagged into error. Twice he got to within one frame of me, with the tension mounting all the time.

Out, damned spot! Shakespeare

Eddie Charlton was trailing 27-25 when the BBC television spotlights on the table caused me problems at the start of the eighth session. The lights were being reflected from the object ball, making it very difficult to judge where it should be hit. The problem was especially acute with long pots and I did not think this was a reasonable handicap in a world championship, especially since these were crowd lights, anyway, and not essential for the cameras covering the play.

For some reason they seemed to bother me more than they did Eddie Charlton, perhaps because the Australian comes from a part of the world where there is a lot more sunshine than we normally enjoy and consequently he is more used to glare, or perhaps he can cope with it better because he has more protuberant eyebrows and more heavily lidded eyes.

Tournament director Bruce Donkin was always close at hand and I asked him, 'Can we do without these spotlights?' He promised to have a word with the television people, but he got no joy there, for they insisted that the lights must stay. I told Bruce Donkin I would play one more frame, then I wanted a meeting to be called, otherwise I would just walk off. The tournament director then warned me that if I refused to play in the conditions that existed I would be disqualified. That made me really livid. I walked off and asked for a meeting in the tournament director's office. Eddie Charlton would have nothing to do with my protest and was not at the meeting, at which the organisers took the word of the television people that the lights were essential for the filming of the final.

I therefore called upon John Mack, managing director of Gallahers Ltd, who was there on behalf of the sponsors. I said to him: 'Mr Mack, whose tournament is this? Is this the Park Drive world professional snooker championship, or is it the television snooker championship?' John Mack made it quite clear that it was the Park Drive championship final, whereupon I told him that I would not continue unless the lights were removed. When the television people saw that I was adamant it suddenly became quite easy to manage without the lights that were bothering me.

The two larger spotlights were extinguished, which made the position tolerable, but the snag was that by now I was not exactly in the right frame of mind for the job at hand. It was at this point that I became indebted once again to the advice of Joe Davis, who had attended the meeting and heard the argument. 'Take a few minutes' break and simmer down before playing again,' Joe advised me. That break to regain my composure did the trick, for my concentration was spot-on again and I was 31-29 ahead when the last day's play began.

So great had been the tension in this final that I had asked Sue to stay away until the last day. Happily, when she arrived she found me full of confidence, with the crisis over. Eddie was the one who cracked on this occasion and I won the afternoon session 5-2, then wrapped up this nerve-racking tournament with a 38-32 victory in the evening.

After a tremendous struggle that had earned me £1,500 I was champion of the world for a second time. In the end the dispute over television lights seemed to act as a spur, for I started the last day with a break of 91. Nothing could quite match the thrill I felt the first time I gained the world crown, but I think I valued it even more this time, for losing it had taught me just how much it meant. I had wanted the title back so much that I prepared for the tournament more thoroughly than I had ever prepared for anything before, walking many miles round snooker tables, at home and elsewhere, playing 182 frames in thirteen days, before the championships started. All that hard work repaid me and one of my supporters did not do too badly out of it either, for he backed me for £200 at my blackest moment and picked up £13,000.

93

Those things denied the prisoner become precisely what he most wants Eldridge Cleaver

England amateur Chris Ross accompanied me in May on another six-week tour of South Africa, with Cape Town, Durban, Johannesburg and Port Elizabeth on the schedule, plus a pro-am tournament. I helped Great Britain beat the Rest of the World in a match in Bradford before we left. Sue and the children joined me in July.

It was during this visit to South Africa that I had my first and only experience of playing in a prison, at Kroonstad in the Orange Free State. One thing is certain: no audience is more hopeful that there will be a break. Residents in this prison had worn out the cloth on their snooker table and had patched it with pieces of shirt and blanket. The cloth had been smoothed with a shirt iron, to the serious detriment of the nap. The cloth was yellow and white, rather than green, and the pockets had been repaired with string. You could say without exaggeration that I found the playing conditions rather strange.

Still, the spectators showed unusual delight in my exhibition and at least they were a captive audience. There was none of the distracting noise a waiter can make while collecting pint pots and not one of the spectators left the room while I was playing.

My brother Ron was in Durban. His visit to South Africa in 1970 was our twenty-first birthday present to him and he stayed in that country as a billiard table fitter. As I played with the children on the beach in 1973, I wondered if I, too, should remain in South Africa.

The fact is that I have never been seriously tempted to emigrate to another country. I thought about the situation, reckoned that I was already able to earn about £30,000 a year and realised that home called strongly. There is only one country for me and I live in it now.

On that tour of South Africa I produced some really remarkable form, knocking up a total of 65 century breaks in the seventeen and a half weeks between 8 May and 9 September 1973. In fact, you can discount six days of that time, for in the middle of

94

June I flew back to England to play in a tournament sponsored by the Myers Bed company, won it and flew back to South Africa to resume my tour. Upon arrival I would have made a good tester for the sponsoring company's products, for I was really tired, but I soon got back into my century-making routine. Here is a list of my 'tons' on that tour:

MAY

8	Wanderers Club	Johannesburg	102
9	Rosewold Club	Johannesburg	100,102
10	Savoy Hotel	Johannesburg	102
13	Mr Elliott	Johannesburg	104
14	Barea Park	Vanderbijal	100
15	Mr Vey	Johannesburg	115, 113
20	Mr Scott	Mondeor	118, 127, 100
21	Metal Box Company	Vanderbijal	129
22	Stewart and Lloyds	Veerenhing	117
23	Benoni Club	Benoni	125
24	USCO Recreation Club	Veerenhing	106
25	SA Club	Krugersdorp	108
26	Mr Chamberlain	Pretoria	105
28	Mr Crook	Johannesburg	105

JUNE

3	Mr Berman	Johannesburg	117
4	Tavistock Colliery	Witbank	103, 129, 104
6	Mr Green	Johannesburg	102
8	West Rand Union	Johannesburg	132, 107
11	Mr Hertsenburg	Johannesburg	111, 118
11	Mr Lang	Johannesburg	136, 115

Return to London for *Make a Break*

19	Green Lantern Inn	Northern Natal	125
20	Kloof CC	Durban	104
22	Royal Hotel	Ladysmith	104
26	Kokstad Club	Equaland	117, 133
29	Iscor Club	Newcastle	100, 102
30	Iscor Club	Newcastle	104

JULY

5	Perrie Mans (match)	Johannesburg	102
6	Transvaal Auto Club	Johannesburg	109
8	Mr McDuling	Johannesburg	113, 115
11	Springs CC	Johannesburg	110
12	Suburbs Club	Johannesburg	104
14	Coal and Iron Club	Hlobane	104, 113
16	Vryheyd Club	Vryheyd	101
20	Mr Ecutt	Durban	107
23	Wanderers Club	Durban	112
25	Lotus Club	Durban	100
27	Iscor Durnacol Club	Natal	129

AUGUST

1	Stellenbosch Club	Cape	118
2	Strand Club	Cape	101
4	Glengaraph Club	Cape	108
5	Mr Scott	Johannesburg	120, 115
8	Elgro Hotel	Free State	124
9	North-West Command Club	Free State	103, 136, 118
10	South African Railways Club	Kroonstad	103
13	Ficksburg Club	Free State	108, 120
18	Mr Elliott	Johannesburg	111
24	Koffiefontein Club	Free State	109
	(Holiday, Durban)		

SEPTEMBER

9	Mr McDuling	Johannesburg	104
10	Return home		

'Tis man's to fight, but heaven's to give success Homer

Century breaks, even on that scale, do not grip the imagination in quite the same way as 'a maximum.' That is the perfect break, a 147, which is to the century break what climbing Everest is to conquering other peaks.

My first maximum was watched by an excited audience of

holiday-makers at Pontins Broadreeds Camp at Selsey-on-Sea, Sussex, with entertainer Charlie Smithers as my opponent on 25 July 1972. I had made a break of 128 on the same table earlier that week, but never before in my career had I managed fifteen reds, fifteen blacks and all the colours. It was a memorable occasion for me too. For my first shot I had to play one red off another into the middle pocket and unfortunately it left the red I had used almost touching the brown, so that it could not be potted into any pocket. With three reds left on the table, one was near the brown and one was touching the pink, but in the end fortune smiled on me and I hit the jackpot.

My second maximum break was scored on 27 September 1973, at Burnt Mill Social Club, Harlow, where earlier in the evening I had made a break of 128 in clearing the table. The worst moment in my maximum break occurred when I potted the blue and failed to remove the pink as far as I intended from its awkward position near a side cushion. The cue ball and the pink finished only about an inch apart, so I played the shot as a sharp tap, with hardly any follow through. The pink was potted and there was still enough strength to take the cue ball round for the black. It left me the job of sinking the black from an acute angle, but down it went.

Four months later, maximum no 3 arrived on Thursday, 31 January 1974, at the Bateson Street Working Men's Club, Leeds, where I was in peak form in a Park Drive exhibition match. On the same visit I made breaks of 80, 84, 68, 67, 115 and 126. Harry Whitby was my opponent when I made my 147.

I had to wait only two weeks for the fourth, while playing John Pulman at the home of George Lock, who is head of precision engineering companies and lives at Bourne End, Buckinghamshire. Once more a certificated referee was in charge and the pockets of the table satisfied the official templates. John Pulman broke off and left me snookered behind the green. I played off the side cushion into the pack, leaving a touching ball. John played away, intending to put me under the baulk cushion again, but he miscued and only reached the side cushion, giving me the chance to put him in trouble. In trying to get out of it he left me with an opening from which I built my maximum. My worst moment on this occasion was when I forgot just how lively was the top cushion and in potting the blue came back much too far down the table for the pink. I had a difficult shot into the top left-hand pocket, but made it and came off the two side cushions behind the black, to send that into the same pocket.

I got my third maximum break in the first one and a half months of 1974 and my fifth overall on 13 February, of all dates, while playing an opponent named Ron Walsh at Ellesmere Port Old Comrades Club. This one equalled Joe Davis's record of five maximum breaks.

I got my sixth maximum at Virginia Water, Surrey, on 14 December 1974, when we were making a 16mm video instructional film. We set up the balls as if the frame had been broken and as chance would have it the whole thing went without a flaw and I built the perfect break. We had formed a company to market the film, but in spite of the maximum it did not go well. We wound up the company in the end and I think I probably lost money, which was a poor end to a great start.

Maximum no 7 is probably unique, for it was made with the yellow ball on 4 March 1976, when I was playing at the Metal Box Company in Vanderbijal, South Africa. During the game I said to the referee, 'There is a hair on the cue ball.' He picked it up, wiped it and replaced it in the same position, whereupon I told him the hair was still there. We had a close look then and realised the ball was cracked.

I still have that cue ball, with two hairline cracks going in opposite directions, which is very unusual. Anyway, we switched the white ball and yellow ball, which is nearest in the colour sequence. The change did not bother me, for using the yellow as the cue ball I made a 147 break. It came in the final frame and earlier I had made two century breaks.

My next maximum was achieved at the home of my good friend Gordon Ingham at South Owram, Halifax, on 1 March 1978.

Just over a year later, on 10 April 1979, one week before the world championship, BBC Wales were filming a documentary and I was playing at Shirley Social Club, Solihull, Birmingham. Conditions were quite ridiculous, especially the lighting, for the glare of the portable spotlights was right in my eyes. Around 9.30 pm, with one frame or so to go, the film crew decided to pop out for a much needed drink. With the spotlights out I took the first ten reds and a black with each, which caused word to be sent to the missing crew. They shot back in a panic, in time to see me complete a maximum. The worst shot was my last, when the white finished to within two inches of the blue spot from where, using the rest, I had cut in the black from its spot. I did it and there was uproar in the place.

It was a crazy occasion altogether, for while I was playing a waitress was going along a row of seats collecting empty glasses and the noise she made was unbelievable. One pocket in the middle of the table was drooping and, to crown it all, after I had completed my maximum someone stole the black ball. I had taken the set of balls with me and the theft spoiled it, but the black ball is a crucial one and will have a value one day, which explains but does not excuse what happened.

Anyone who could collect all the black balls that have been used in the world championship finals, or have figured in maximum breaks, would have something worth a lot of money. Not many people realise that you can buy almost anything at the major events, even the cloth off the table.

Three weeks later I got my tenth maximum, at East Birmingham Trades Club, Saltley. I scored two maximum breaks in practice at home and I count them, for they were genuine in every respect. Other people may quibble about them, but as far as I am concerned those breaks were as good as any.

My thirteenth maximum break was made at Perth Tennis Club on 13 June 1981, when playing against Raymond Clive Miquel, chairman and managing director of Bell's Scotch Whisky. It was also my 3,049th century break. There was another special feature of this maximum, as I will recount later.

My best tournament break was one short of the maximum, on 18 October 1972, at Dial House Sports Club, Sheffield, where the top break was worth £1 a point and there was a bonus for a century. When there were only three reds left I was confronted by a pink that was a Bank of England shot or a slightly chancey black. I elected to be sure rather than sorry, so I finished up with the money and a 146 and not a 147.

Television camera crews have been unlucky on several occasions, apart from the one I have mentioned at the Shirley Social Club in 1979. The most notable occurred when John Spencer achieved a maximum while playing in a tournament at Slough Community Centre in the same year. Again the cameramen had nipped out for refreshment. They were not neglecting their duty, it was just that they were not destined to capture that particular magic moment on film.

Of course there were no cameras around when Joe Davis set the world record with a maximum break in 1955, or when Rex Williams equalled the feat ten years later. There was a change of luck for television at the Crucible Theatre in Sheffield in the 1981 championships when Doug Mountjoy hit me with a break of 145. Until then relatively few people had seen a performance of that kind and it provided a treat for the watching millions. Doug decided to take a blue at one point in the break and deprived himself of the chance of picking up the £10,000 prize that goes with achieving a maximum break in a tournament.

Promoters have to insure against such a contingency, for while a maximum break is a thrill for everyone who sees it compiled, it can take the gilt off the financial gingerbread. I can sympathise with Doug for getting so close, even though I was on the wrong end of the performance.

It did not do a lot for my confidence at the time, but I did enjoy his triumph. The fact is that after the first ten blacks had gone down the frame was as good as over.

Behaviour is a mirror in which everyone displays his own image
Goethe

March 1974 brought me an unexpected visit to India at short notice. Alex Higgins was the man responsible, since he had

100

gone out there, ignored the old rule that in Rome you do as the Romans do and was put on the plane back home after only one game. He made a century break in that one game, but in typical Alex Higgins style, he did it without wearing a shirt. Going topless was the Higgins answer to the oppressive heat and he was apparently oblivious to the fact that social standards in the places in which he was due to play in India are nothing like as relaxed as they are in clubs on a tour back home in England. I doubt if there are many clubs in Britain who would take kindly to a visiting star playing without wearing his shirt, though they might possibly make an exception in the case of a female player. As far as the men are concerned the clubs expect and appreciate the bow tie image. Alex has always been something of a rebel in the matter of dress, as in other ways, and he left behind him in India some ruffled feathers. He can rarely have been further out of line, for social gaffes of this kind are not tolerated in the best of circles in India.

I was asked to fly out there to complete the scheduled tour and generally to try to smooth things over. I arrived on 11 March and on the first day made breaks of 98 and 101 at the West India Automobile Association Club in Bombay. On 17 March I made another century break, a 105 in Bangalore and five days later produced the biggest break ever made in India, a 136 at Nungambakkam Stadium in Madras. The following day, 23 March, I made two century breaks, 102 and 127, in Madras and Calcutta. I finished with a 125 on 25 March, also in Calcutta.

During my seventeen day trip I did as much sightseeing as I could, including the obligatory visit to see the wonderful Taj Mahal, which I very much enjoyed, but India as a whole did not suit me at all. I found the extremes of affluence and poverty hard to bear and the conditions in which some of the people existed in some places was most distressing. In saying that, I keep in mind the fact that I was only in the country for seventeen days and that is nowhere near long enough to form a considered judgement on a land as big as India.

Back I went to England for the Park Drive world championships in the Central and Lancaster Halls, Belle Vue, Manchester. After India there could hardly be a more complete change of environment, though by now such things did not bother me at all. Wherever I was, if I started to miss a few shots, I would say to myself: 'Come on, you are supposed to be champion. You shouldn't be missing these.' Some of the critics were saying that in the previous twelve months I had been playing as well as anyone had ever played snooker. Be that as it may, I notched my third world championship.

This time there was £10,000 in prize-money at stake and in my half of the draw were Eddie Charlton, who was runner-up the previous year, Alex Higgins, Marcus Owen, Fred Davis and Jim Meadowcroft, my second round opponent, who had beaten Kingsley Kennerley 8-5 in round one. I beat Jim Meadowcroft 15-3. (Frame scores: 76-48, 72-65, 40-61, 71-34, 71-53, 57-21, 73-46, 99-28, 81-34, 42-88, 69-49, 60-31, 100-38, 91-36, 78-44, 82-33, 17-59, 100-17.) My best break was a 73 in the thirteenth frame.

My quarter-final opponent was Marcus Owen, who was a Walthamstow window cleaner when we last met when he beat me 6-1 in the Southern Area amateur final of 1967. We were on one of the outside tables, where there was more noise and movement, but little atmosphere. I wanted revenge, but things did not look too promising when Marcus finished the first session 4-3 ahead and had made a break of 102. After that, his anxiety showed at times and he made errors that enabled me to lead 8-4, before he hauled me back to 8-8. I was 11-10 in front at the start of the final session and took four of the last five frames to win 15-11. (Frame scores (mine first): 77-60, 41-58, 59-42, 60-39, 97-14, 14-102, 54-68, 78-52, 73-41, 56-47, 96-17, 87-16, 37-70, 54-65, 20-93, 31-57, 102-34, 92-22, 25-68, 96-28, 19-88, 77-37, 73-5, 77-9, 68-73, 83-18.)

My old rival Fred Davis, from Stourport, was the semifinal opponent and after five close frames I romped away to win 15-3. (Frame scores: 75-31, 26-104, 58-49, 47-61, 75-36, 67-58, 57-55, 35-72, 71-23, 68-48, 72-61, 58-43, 85-8, 93-15, 88-26, 107-16, 58-52 85-29.)

There had been some big shocks in these championships, for Perrie Mans put out John Spencer in the second round and forty-seven year old Yorkshireman John Dunning put paid to the hopes of Eddie Charlton, while Fred Davis had beaten Alex Higgins in a quarter-final, so my opponent in the final was Graham Miles, of Birmingham. Possibly because Manchester is within easy commuting distance of my home and I was able to return there each night and leave all tensions behind me, I was in as relaxed a frame of mind as I have ever been for a major event and I won the best-of-forty-three frames final 22-12.

I made my usual afternoon start by trailing 2-0 and Graham Miles had a break of 101 before I forged 4-3 in front by the end of the session. I started the next day 9-5 ahead and took five of the next six to lead 14-7 at the start of the evening session on the second day. This fell flat and I was pulled back to 17-11, which was warning enough. On the morning of the third day I won 5-1 to clinch victory. (Frame scores (mine first): 59-68, 31-64, 58-45, 94-27, 5-101, 92-31, 71-37, 81-52, 102-25, 63-64, 78-48, 70-36, 22-81, 68-42, 19-95, 99-7, 93-45, 78-34, 28-64, 100-31, 99-13, 78-14, 51-64, 52-61, 68-75, 61-25, 54-64, 110-23, 91-26, 63-36, 82-9, 45-80, 81-44, 74-61.) My best break was 97 in the twenty-first frame.

I did not rate my form anything more than mediocre, perhaps because I was never put under real pressure. I did not feel the elation of the previous victories, in fact it was a bit of an anticlimax, for I had expected a titanic struggle. I think Graham Miles was shattered by his struggle to reach the final and was affected a bit by the occasion.

Still, I treasured the comments of seventy-three year old maestro Joe Davis, who was kind enough to say of me: 'He is a great credit to the profession. I could not give him advice. He does it all perfectly.' Praise indeed from a man of such renown.

For the apparel oft proclaims the man   Shakespeare

I have a special reason for remembering the 1974 final. I had a sponsor, Marsden's Tailors, of Stoke-on-Trent, and they provided me with nine jackets, so that I could wear a different one with dress suit trousers each night. They were all very distinctive jackets: pink, stripes, loud squares and quiet squares. It all became a bit of a gimmick with the men from the media. I made a practice of keeping on my overcoat until the last minute, to keep them guessing as to what would be the rig of the day.

It was all good fun and on the final night there had to be something special. It was a jacket in scarlet silk, far too striking to be covered by a mere overcoat. I decided to go the whole hog and wear a top hat and cape. The image was intended to be a touch of the Champagne Charlies, but it did not quite work out that way. I still get echoes of that night, for someone decided the outfit made me look like Dracula and that name stuck to me more than most. Perhaps it was just that the gear made me resemble the infamous count, or it could be that my opponents reckoned there was no stopping me once I had tasted blood.

Anyway, the name has lingered much longer than the others: the Young Banger title of my boyhood in Tredegar, the Chief Inspector tag I got in memory of my police service, at the time I first became world champion, or the daftest of all, in New Zealand. I was playing in the Saccones 10,000 dollars world snooker classic in October and November of 1974, when I was billed as The Welsh Corgi. Though I would obviously have to admit to the Welsh bit, I cannot explain the corgi part, unless it is that this breed of dog has been known to bite in the highest circles, like Dracula. Luckily names do not bother me, or there might be blood for supper, as they say in the Potteries.

9
ASTRIDE THE WORLD

Every man wants to appear considerable in his native place
Samuel Johnson

On 24 April 1974, I received an honour that touched me deeply.
I was elected as South Wales Sportsman of the Year and at a
miners gala in the Sophia Gardens in Cardiff I received a miniature version of a miner's lamp. It has a place of honour in my
home and is a constant reminder of my origins. Nothing matters more than being acknowledged by your own people. I also
had a miniature version of a miner's lamp from my former
workmates at Florence Colliery in Stoke-on-Trent and I keep
the two together as mementoes with which I will never part.

This was the year when Pontins introduced their snooker
festival at Prestatyn, with 398 amateurs and eight professionals
in the open tournament. Like John Spencer I found that I could
not give former Welsh miner Doug Mountjoy 25 start and he
beat me in the semifinal. He went on to meet and beat John
Spencer in the final and win £1,000, plus a continental holiday.
Still, there was also a professional tournament, in which I won
the £1,000 prize, beating Fred Davis 9-4, Cliff Thorburn 8-5
and John Spencer 10-9 in a tremendous final. It was a fine start
to a most popular tournament.

One of my most important trips of this period was made with
Eddie Charlton, when we set out to promote the game in the
Southern Hemisphere. We travelled thousands of miles, playing seven days a week in New Zealand. I finished on top in that
tour and made a break of 102 in Palmerston North in a £5,000
match with Eddie.

Flying is the safest method of travel and I love it, in fact there are times when I wish I had been equipped with wings, but the fact is that when you fly you are in the hands of the pilot and I always make a practice on long distance journeys of getting anaesthetised with drink.

There was one trip with Eddie when this did not happen. We had a busy schedule in Australia and were travelling from Cooma, up in the Snowy Mountains, to Sydney. The snag was that our luggage was not on the same flight and while we waited for it to catch up with us we had a helicopter standing by to whisk us to the Croydon motel from Tullamarine airport in Melbourne.

This involved a cross-country flight of about fifteen miles and when the helicopter got up to about 1,000ft the door suddenly flew open. 'What the . . . .!' exclaimed the pilot, who quickly tried to compensate for having inadvertently added to the alarm by saying, 'No need to panic.' As far as I was concerned he was too late with his reassurance, but I tried not to show it and we made our trip safely, with the body cooler than the mind. We were on our way to play a match in the Nunawading Basketball Stadium, to raise money for a third court there.

My family are no strangers to the sort of heart-stopping experience you can have when problems arise during flights of this kind, as distinct from the operations of normal airlines. Once when Sue, Darren and Melanie were staying with me at the Park Hotel in Durban, South Africa, the owner Carl Erasmus, flew us in his private Cessna aircraft to a game reserve about 100 miles away. It was intended mainly as a treat for the children, but we ran into local bad weather and were bucked about alarmingly. Luckily we all took it quite well and did not disgrace ourselves, but you do tend to remember such incidents quite vividly.

One of my odd memories of a visit to Australia concerns a game of golf on a course at Wyalla, near Adelaide. The fairways were rocky and barren, so that when I got to the first tee and looked towards the flag I was more curious than surprised to see a black patch. It was the first black green I had ever seen, if you can have so obvious a contradiction in terms. The putting sur-

Memories of my home town were brought back by this street scene of
Tredegar. The painting was presented to me at a civic reception in 1978 in
generous recognition of my snooker achievements

(*Above*) Scoring the magic 'maximum' of 147 is always a thrill. This was the occasion of my eighth maximum break at the home of Gordon Ingham (on my right) in Sheffield. (*Below*) A black pot for a Pot Black champion! A gift from Portmeirion Potteries in Stoke-on-Trent after I had won the BBC tournament in 1979

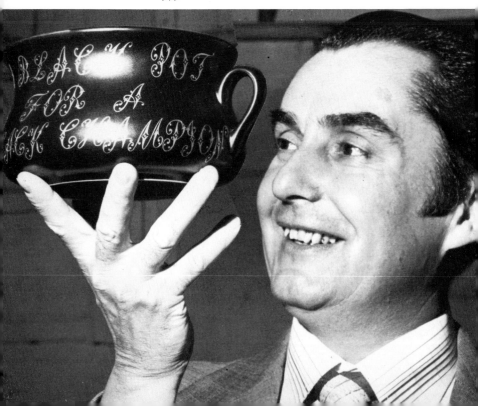

face was made from coal dust, treated to make it slightly tacky. I was no stranger to coal dust, as you know, but I never imagined I would see it used as a putting surface for golf.

When I got back home I played in the Norwich Union open snooker competition and reached the final, in which I lost 10-9 to John Spencer, who won £1,400. I got half that amount, plus an extra £100 for the highest break, one of 130.

Stoke-on-Trent made their third presentation to me that December. The Lord Mayor, Harry Smallwood, handed over to me a trophy the City Council had ordered from Henry Pidduck and Sons Ltd, the Hanley jewellers. It was specially designed by them and made by local craftsmen. The plinth is a replica of a snooker table and on it is a triangle, resting on black and white snooker balls, supported by crossed cues.

At this stage of my career I felt on top of the world, more confident than I had been before or have been since. I knew that as long as I played to my best form, no one in the world would beat me. I had just defeated Manchester's Dave Taylor in the Watney Mann tournament in Manchester, with the help of five century breaks. Oddly enough, though Britain was not exactly brimming over with world champions, I did not rate an invitation to the BBC Television Sportsman of the Year awards night. In point of fact I hardly gave the matter a thought, but Stoke-on-Trent South Member of Parliament Jack Ashley took up the cudgels on my behalf, complaining that it was a snub.

Snooker's rise in social status was amply illustrated by a dinner jacket, champagne and smoked salmon setting for the Benson and Hedges Masters tournament in January 1975, held at the West Centre Hotel, Fulham, with a first prize of £2,000. I beat Pot Black champion Graham Miles 5-3 and Rex Williams by the same score, then lost 9-8 to John Spencer in a thrilling final on a re-spotted black.

The same month I beat Jackie Rea in a Dublin church hall to win the Irish title.

Few of us can stand prosperity, another man's I mean

Mark Twain

For only the third time in its history, the world professional snooker championship was staged overseas in April 1975, Australian sponsors having an offer of £18,900 accepted by the World Professional Billiards and Snooker Association, of which Rex Williams was chairman and I was vice-chairman.

Free air fares were offered for the professional champions of South Africa and Canada and for six British players. As title holder I was an automatic choice, along with the runner-up, Graham Miles, and the two beaten semifinalists, Fred Davis and Rex Williams. Though he had been knocked out in the second round the previous year, John Spencer had the kind of record that entitled him to one of the other two invitations and the other went to John Pulman, by special request of the Australians. John Dunning was nominated as first reserve. There was no place for Alex Higgins, bedevilled by non-snooker factors and left to pay his own way.

I had played in public almost every day over the previous five years and I decided upon a rather different kind of preparation for the championship in Australia. I just let myself go, had some late nights, threw a couple of parties and had a lot more to drink than I usually do. When I got back to snooker I felt a bit rusty at first, but the touch soon came back, I felt fresh and keen and I believe that week's break was an inspiration.

My first match was in the second round against Warren Simpson, the Australian, at Gosford in New South Wales, on the best table I encountered in Australia, an old fashioned eight-legger. I won each of the first three sessions 4-3 to lead 12-9, then clinched it at 15-11. (Frame scores (mine first): 72-35, 15-77, 65-50, 69-44, 42-89, 67-44, 42-89, 67-44, 13-119, 64-52, 59-73, 86-11, 60-50, 62-69, 108-38, 36-76, 82-32, 10-107, 14-88, 68-61, 86-32, 85-29, 52-59, 84-49, 94,26, 10-83, 70-80, 78-31.)

After our battle in the quarter-final, both John Spencer and I agreed that it was probably the greatest snooker match ever played. Certainly I had never potted better or defended better.

Before I tell you about it though, ask yourself how they worked it out.

John Spencer was seeded no 8, which takes a bit of understanding when you consider that he had been world champion twice and had beaten me twice in major tournaments that season. The explanation I received was that the seedings were decided on the previous year's championship, in which John lost in the last 16 to Perrie Mans. Even then, the system was not followed strictly. In fact, not to put too fine a point on it, the seedings were a farce and the World Professional Billiards and Snooker Association changed the system a few months later.

John Spencer made it hot for me from the start, with breaks of 103 and 114 in the opening session, which he won 4-2. I took the last two frames of the first day to restrict his lead to 7-5. In the next session John was 3-1 ahead and I drew level at 3-3. I came good and actually got one ahead in the evening session, but we finished level at 12-12 overall. We split the third afternoon session 3-3 and the decisive moment came in the final one, with John leading 17-16. He was a few in front when he took the second last red and the green, screwing down for the last red that was half hidden by the pink. He was a quarter of an inch too far to be able to pot it and if he had won that frame he would have been two up with three to go. As it was I took the frame to level at 17-17 and the next two to win the quarter-final 19-17. (Frame scores: 68-48, 20-103, 43-76, 7-121, 62-75, 63-54, 36-89, 30-75, 83-15, 56-67, 91-6, 91-23, 0-123, 91-0, 4-117, 50-69, 80-43, 75-56, 49-76, 99-27, 73-67, 71-8, 80-54, 34-87, 82-49, 20-67, 43-79, 67-30, 87-18, 33-81, 39-102, 73-8, 63-70, 79-50, 56-36, 53-10.)

I lost count of the number of games that were won from 50 or 60 behind, but there must have been a dozen. It was such a nail-biter that we both might have finished up looking like Admiral Lord Nelson. My highest break was a 60.

My opponent in the semifinals was Alex Higgins, who had made the trip under his own steam. I had him under pressure from the start, winning the opening sessions 5-1 and 4-2. You cannot write off Alex though, and he took the second afternoon session 5-1 and in the evening drew level at 10-10. I claimed the next four frames, two of them on the black, but it left me 14-10 in front. Alex took the afternoon session of the third day 4-2 to make it 16-14, but I claimed the first three of the evening session to win the semifinal 19-14. (Frame scores: 86-29, 7-26, 15-106, 16-83, 68-15, 102-23, 71-64, 83-2, 81-42, 49-62, 69-61, 89-44, 48-64, 60-69, 8-93, 36-83, 41-68, 62-19, 57-61, 35-87, 77-5, 69-59, 69-62, 61-17, 14-62, 56-5, 51-77, 60-26, 24-88, 57-67, 52-14, 83-17, 73-43.) Alex had the best break of 83 and I had a 66 in the first frame. I thought Alex played quite well and few people appreciate the skill with which he negotiates the baulk colours safely.

Eddie Charlton had beaten Dennis Taylor 19-12 in the other semifinal to secure the chance to win the title for the first time and in front of his home crowd, at the Nunawading Basketball Stadium in Melbourne. We ended the first day level at 6-6, with Eddie four times in the lead and me ahead twice. On the second day I took the afternoon session 6-0 and the evening one 4-2 to lead 16-8, so that Eddie, eight frames adrift, looked as good as dead. This tough ex-boxer is not like that, so he won all six frames on the third afternoon and stretched his winning run to nine frames by taking the first three in the evening, which left him 17-16 ahead, which must rank among the best fightbacks the game has ever produced. He played well and had the run of the ball, while I did not help my cause by missing a few middle pocket shots. On this type of table I had trouble whenever I had to bridge on the cushion, especially near a pocket. I also found the top cushion was lively and the baulk cushion slow, the cloth on the table a little on the thick side and the bed of the table medium paced and true.

However, the world's top players have to learn to adapt to any table and the fact was that Eddie was striking the ball very well. He was the finest plain ball player I had ever seen and his cueing was as true as a bullet. He potted an amazing number of balls when he was on the baulk cushion, particularly when the object ball was anything between half an inch and eight inches from the side rail and three to four feet from the top pocket. He potted them and ran through off the side and top cushions for the black.

I managed to win the remaining three frames of the third evening to lead 19-17 and I made it 22-20 on the fourth afternoon. Then Eddie came at me again. He won 5-1 on the fourth evening to lead 25-23 overnight, then took the first four frames on the last day to go 28-23 ahead, making it a sequence of eight wins in a row. I won the last two frames of the session, making breaks of 60 and 59. I cleared the table in the last frame with the help of a neck-or-nothing pink into the top left pocket. If I had missed it Eddie would have needed only one of the last seven frames to claim the world title that has always eluded him. When the pink went down, Eddie wilted visibly.

His normally unshakable confidence took a further blow in the first frame of the final session. He was 22 ahead with only four colours left, having potted the green in superb and daring fashion. He left himself a simple task of potting the brown from its spot, something he would normally do ninety-nine times out of a hundred. This time the tension affected him, as it affects all of us on occasions and he left the brown in the jaws of the pocket, so that I was able to mop up the remaining colours. I lost the toss for the respotted black and left Eddie a half-chance, but he over-cut and left the black in the middle of the baulk cushion. I over-hit a tricky safety shot leaving a difficult chance.

The cue ball was tight under the side cushion and Eddie was again too thin with his shot, so that the cue ball flashed into the baulk pocket to give me the frame. There was still a long way to go, but psychologically I felt I was home and dry. I won four successive frames to extend my winning run to seven and lead 30-29, making a break of 92 in the process, but battling Eddie drew level again, making it a last frame decider. Twice he had me in terrible trouble in one of the baulk corners and the only way I could get back down the table was by going in-off. Two in-offs brought the scores to 16-16, then I managed to piece together a break of 62 to take the £4,000 first prize by winning the title for a fourth time. This win also completed my hat trick of victories in the championship.

113

I was very proud of this one, for as they say in boxing, you have to knock your man out in Australia to get a draw. The seedings had been absolutely ridiculous, with all the top players in my half of the draw. It made my win a bit special and now I was in demand all over the world. (Frame scores in the final, which I won 31-30: 2-84, 60-59, 49-65, 93-25, 103-25, 42-69, 87-21, 19-84, 33-67, 81-30, 9-86, 64-63, 65-47, 80-46, 66-56, 64-51, 115-16, 82-20, 39-69, 28-96, 76-55, 64-20, 121-14, 115-2, 38-86, 43-77, 27-101, 45-69, 32-59, 46-95, 29-68, 2-64, 12-55, 68-53, 72-47, 57-50, 52-60, 54-52, 25-72, 59-30, 68-23, 10-110, 50-68, 75-15, 26-79, 49-69, 50-68, 18-66, 55-99, 52-54, 22-70, 34-74, 92-7, 71-64, 73-66, 75-37, 60-26, 76-5, 11-16, 51-97, 84-18.)

Three days after playing in the world final in Melbourne I was in Prestatyn, Wales, for the second Pontins Festival of Snooker, which this time attracted 657 amateur entries. In the open tournament the amateurs play down to the last 24, at which stage they are joined by the eight professionals, who give 25 start.

I started in the professional tournament with a first round match with Graham Miles, in which I was 4-1 and 5-3 in front and only won 7-6. I went on to beat Cliff Thorburn 7-4 and John Spencer 10-4, in the latter match coming from behind in both morning and afternoon sessions to win 5-2 and 4-2. John made a break of 117 in pulling back from 9-2 to 9-4, but I took the next frame to win. In the semifinals I beat Cliff Thorburn 7-4 and John Spencer beat Rex Williams 7-5. In the final I beat John Spencer 10-4 to take the £1,000.

Then it was the pro-am in a taxing week after the world championships, for in the last three days at Pontins I was playing morning, afternoon and night. In the last 32 I had to give Terry Griffiths, of Llanelli, 25 start and I beat him 4-1. He has since, of course, won the world professional title. Next came Lance Pibworth, a methodical left-hander from Bedworth, who quickly went 3-0 ahead. This amateur, who plays with a glove on his bridge hand to combat clamminess, did not enter the national championship because he did not think he could win.

Anyway, he made me fight all out to win 4-3.

My quarter-final opponent was another left-hander, Maurice Chapman, the former Midland champion, who also had me in desperate trouble. He led me 1-0, 2-1, 3-2 and I missed at least three blacks off the spot as weariness took its toll, but I cleared the colours to win the sixth off the black and after being 63-0 down, had a break of 47 in winning the decider, again on the black. Chapman missed a thin cut blue for the match, which I won 4-3.

There were 1,500 people in their seats by 10.30 am to see my semifinal clash with Patsy Fagan, of High Wycombe. The young Irishman had a contingent of London supporters and had the bulk of the female backing, but despite having 25 start and leading 3-0, he lost 4-3.

Perhaps the support affected his performance. I needed a snooker on the colours in the first frame and got it, then left the pink over a pocket. In the second I trailed 40 behind with two reds left, yet should have won it before giving it away by leaving the brown over the pocket. Then Patsy Fagan made it 3-0 and I pulled him back to 3-3, winning the fifth frame on the black and the sixth on the pink. In the final frame I was guilty of a very bad miss, but Patsy missed three of a like nature and I beat him. (Frame scores: 57-75, 46-81, 58-73, 85-91, 68-55, 75-62, 89-61.)

John Virgo was the other finalist and I beat him 7-1, taking no chances. I won the first frame on the black and the second on the pink, after John had led 61-0. I was 5-0 ahead before he won a frame. (The scores were: 65-59, 86-69, 84-44, 90-56, 95-60, 33-83, 72-48, 82-61.) I had breaks of 62 and 46. John Virgo seemed to lose his confidence and it allowed me to win a further £1,000, to make it £6,000 in little over a week.

At home everyone in the family was at Loggerheads, though there was no disharmony. Loggerheads is a village just over the Staffordshire border into Shropshire and that was where we were living. I was not there as often as I would have liked and often wished I could spend more time with Sue and the children, who were growing up fast in my absence. I would have liked to have seen more major events staged nearer my home and to test the market visits were made first by John Spencer, then Alex Higgins, to play matches with me for a Lancia car. The idea was to build up a following for snooker in plush surroundings, but neither night gave much encouragement to the promoters and I was greeted by so many friends that I found it very hard indeed to do myself justice.

There was a shock for me in December 1975, when I returned to my car, which I had parked in Curzon Street in London. A thief had raided the car and had taken about £300 worth of my property. To my very great relief he had left behind the one thing that was irreplaceable, my precious cue. Seeing it safe and sound softened the blow of my other losses.

Next came a six week tour of Australia with Eddie Charlton, who was eight frames ahead before I beat him 125-122. We played an additional week-long match, which I also won. Eddie had the best break of the series, a 136, but I had a 131 and a 113 at Belmont, near Newcastle, New South Wales, which comprised fifteen reds and fourteen blacks. The fifteenth black was left teetering over the edge of the pocket and I believe I would have had another 147 maximum had it dropped.

Strive mightily, but eat and drink as friends   Shakespeare

The following January I was involved in a recording session at Thames Television Ladbroke international series at the Holiday Inn in London when I heard Eamonn Andrews say, 'Ray Reardon, This is Your Life.' Many times I have heard people discuss whether the 'victim' is really surprised when this happens, but I can assure you that I had no inkling of what was about to happen. I felt as surprised as I looked.

John Pulman, John Spencer and Graham Miles were there, along with Cliff Thorburn, of Canada, Jackie Rea and Alex Higgins, of Ireland, Eddie Charlton, from Australia, Joe Davis and seven-times women's champion Joyce Gardner. Eamonn Andrews had arranged for my brother Ron to fly over from Johannesburg, and old colleagues from my mining and police days were there to add their reminiscence. I lived it all over again: marbles on the kitchen table, threats of a spanking for playing for money, Jack Window chauffeuring me around in the old Gutless Wonder, my pit accident and my police service. At home I have a video recording of the show and savour all the emotions again.

Being featured in such a programme is an experience you never forget and I think I am very fortunate to have access to this and other television highlights at the flick of a switch. I was playing in Jersey, staying with personal friends, Barry and Jean Woolf, a week after the show and was amazed by people who stopped me in the street and in shops. They even made me an honorary member of the exclusive Le Moye Golf Club in Jersey, which was a bonus I never expected. There was another world champion from the Rhondda Valley in the Channel Islands at the same time, darts star Alan Evans, and it seemed to me that we made quite an impression.

The second Benson and Hedges Masters tournament was played at a new venue, the New London Theatre, with a 1,500 seat arena, which was quite often filled. My first encounter was with John Pulman, whom I beat 4-1 in a dreadful match. (Scores were: 61-43, 19-64, 67-51, 56-49, 80-33.) Some of the spectators had paid £12 for a £1.50 ticket, expecting a classic, but we made many errors. John contributed more of them than I did.

That win took me into the semifinals to meet Eddie Charlton and I beat him 5-4. (Scores were: 87-17, 64-23, 77-24, 17-84, 25-79, 0-110, 63-13, 60-68, 62-33.) Eddie could not get going in the first three frames, but he pulled me back to 3-3. Then it was 4-4 and I took the decider, to qualify for the final against Graham Miles. I got off to a great start and was soon leading 5-1. I cleared the table with a break of 90 in the opening session in the evening to make it 6-2 and Graham never really threatened. I picked up £2,000 and he got £1,000. (Frame scores: 79-34, 88-11, 63-1, 42-68, 73-18, 61-22, 41-95, 104-17, 11-85, 57-16.)

Next came a three-week tour of South Africa, during which I made a maximum at the Metal Box Club near Johannesburg, after breaks of 113 and 136. I beat Perrie Mans 8-4 in a special challenge match at Sturrock Park. People in Britain would be envious of some of the facilities in South Africa, especially the Wanderers Club in Johannesburg.

This club was founded in 1887 and has more than 11,000 members, with provision for sixteen sports: athletics, badminton, baseball, bowls for men and women (separate), billiards and snooker, cricket to Test standard, eighteen holes golf, gymnastics, hockey for men and women (separate), rugby, soccer, squash, swimming, table tennis, plus twenty-six tennis courts offering all types of surface, many all-weather. There is also a Japanese garden, restaurant and ballroom.

Those who live more normal lives and have nine-to-five jobs may not class some of my activities as work, but I was maintaining a most exacting schedule and still having to try to play to form. I got home from South Africa about 5 am on the Sunday morning, left early next morning to play celebrity golf at Stoke Poges with Ed (Stewpot) Stewart, got home again about 9 pm and was up at 5 am on the Tuesday to fly to Glasgow; was able to return home briefly on the Thursday morning, before travelling first to Birmingham, then on to Middlesbrough to defend my world title.

10
ACCUSED OF HISTRIONICS

We resent little provocations   William Hazlitt

Quarter-finals in the 1976 Embassy world professional championship were played at two venues, Middlesbrough Town Hall and Wythenshawe Forum, Manchester. My first opponent, John Dunning, of Morley, was playing in his native Yorkshire. I would have preferred to be playing in Manchester, because I could then go home each night.

I lost the first session against John Dunning 4-2, then won thirteen of the next sixteen frames. It was very difficult to concentrate, with a constant stream of people going to and from the bar, toilet and refreshment rooms. Now and then a spectator would light a cigarette right in the player's line of sight and after a protest people were not allowed on the second day to take their glasses and drink into the match arena, which probably curbed the attendance.

Twice in the first frame I had to stand up when potting a pink into the middle pocket because of the moving background of a programme seller's white blouse, but I did manage a break of 81. That made it 1-0, but I still ended the session 4-2 down. In the evening session I took five frames in a row to make it 7-4, apart from making a 106 break. It was 8-6 overnight and I had a 71 break in the sixteenth frame on the way to a 15-7 win. (Frame scores: 88-1, 33-79, 41-46, 79-32, 40-80, 35-81, 80-32, 80-40, 106-0, 86-21, 79-36, 13-93, 74-37, 33-73, 82-27, 71-63, 57-74, 67-46, 91-2, 63-49, 85-42, 98-9.)

Next came Dennis Taylor and he did not give me the fight I expected as I cruised to a 15-2 victory. (Frame scores: 75-50, 101-31, 101-19, 57-41, 80-28, 80-39, 77-47, 20-71, 95-47, 91-38,

72-36, 23-69, 104-12, 69-58, 95-26, 74-49, 115-3.) I had a break of 115 in the last frame.

Perrie Mans, who became the first South African ever to reach the semifinals, was my next obstacle and I beat him 20-10, including a break of 133. I led 4-2 and 8-5, then 12-7, before running into top form and opening up an eight-frame gap. Perrie wilted and I needed only four of the remaining thirteen frames, the first of which I took 133-1. (Frame scores: 42-67, 57-55, 113-8, 56-40, 1-78, 55-53, 31-63, 128-15, 69-37, 19-83, 109-9, 54-71, 64-41, 31-79, 84-30, 77-45, 14-68, 78-24, 89-41, 124-15, 105-27, 95-31, 71-66, 49-63, 63-8, 29-107, 133-1, 6-92, 82-38, 84-46.)

It should be said that the splitting of the championships into two venues was not a success and the crowds at Middlesbrough were very disappointing. Matches were a bit one sided and I was involved in quite a bit of controversy. Drinking means glasses and noise, plus a good deal of movement at the wrong moment. Smoking is forbidden for spectators at most major tournaments, which may be unfair, since a lot of players smoke, including me.

Perhaps those who have witnessed on television how the game can expose the raw ends of nerves when the pressure is on will forgive what seems to be a case of blatant discrimination. Anyway, players when they are smoking are careful not to upset their opponent. When you tour round the clubs you learn to tolerate many things, but the situation is not the same when a world title is at stake.

This was a controversial championship, for the troubles were not yet over. The final at Wythenshawe Forum against Alex Higgins was as notable for the off-the-table distractions as for anything else. I had been playing in Middlesbrough and Alex was familiar with the Forum, since he had been in that half of the draw, so the promoter ordered that the slate and cloth be changed to cancel out his advantage in the final.

Television lights had been installed just before the final began and they were not up to the standard of those at the New London Theatre. The glare and dazzle made distance and angled shots extremely hazardous. What was bound to be a war of nerves was made worse by the fact that the table was not level. There had been a bit of fun at Middlesbrough when the referee called the score, 'Perry Mason 24, Ronald Reardon 21,' and I had my fun at the Forum by declaring that I was having to allow for the wind when making my shots, but the fact was that conditions were far from right. I even had problems with the referee, who subsequently withdrew through back trouble.

I was 4-2 down in the first session and it might have been worse. After the television lights had been adjusted I won five in a row and went 8-5 ahead. Next we had the upset over the level of the table and Alex won five of the first six frames in the following session and went 10-9 ahead. It was my turn again and I took six of the seven frames in the fourth session to lead 15-11. I played cautiously while Alex was brilliant, but erratic. We were 15-13 to me and I was trailing to a 68 break when Alex missed a simple red and let me in to take the frame.

I took the next despite needing a snooker with all the colours left and I built my lead to 19-13, which was virtually unassailable. In the sixth session I extended my lead to 24-15 and needed only three more from the seventh and final session. I clinched it 27-16. I was accused of histrionics, but I won the £6,000 first prize and my fourth consecutive world title, which was the fifth overall. There had been tensions and I was glad I was able to travel home at night and get rid of some of them. Alex Higgins battled very hard and his behaviour was beyond reproach.

(Frame scores: 42-63, 11-62, 66-59, 12-85, 58-17, 6-118, 97-19, 93-32, 101-34, 64-40, 94-15, 32-68, 61-30, 14-95, 17-72, 19-58, 61-19, 20-95, 26-47, 68-41, 32-101, 79-44, 73-35, 102-5, 70-33, 96-21, 32-61, 7-77, 72-68, 64-44, 64-62, 70-48, 71-10, 62-32, 18-90, 53-44, 53-8, 16-56, 58-20, 77-59, 32-75, 82-36, 62-25.)

Next stop was Prestatyn and the Pontins Festival, in which I won another £1,000 in the professional competition. I started in great style against Dennis Taylor and was 6-1 up before the Irishman got going. In one frame I took blacks with the first fourteen reds, then flicked the last red on to a cushion. This quarter-final finished 7-4 and I had breaks of 92, 43, 49, 51, 40, 47, 65.

Next came John Spencer, who was very much out of touch and lost 7-3. My best breaks were 59, 70, 51. Fred Davis was a different proposition in the final and took me to 10-9. He led 3-0 and 4-2, displaying vintage form, so after the first interval I got down to business with a break of 123. In the last but one frame of this session I got a snooker with only one red remaining and went on to clear the table. I went to 8-5 ahead in the next session, then Fred produced a break of 107 to clear the table and he stretched it to a lead of 9-8. I drew level, was 46-6 ahead in the deciding frame and missed a black, with the cue ball under a cushion.

Fred got to 32 and needed only the brown and the blue to win, but he missed an easy brown from the spot and I got a last-gasp win. (Frame scores: 50-72, 38-73, 27-85, 99-5, 96-8, 42-80, 135-1, 66-14, 45-84, 81-37, 71-70, 73-59, 68-34, 30-107, 48-78, 42-75, 50-83, 85-44, 66-47.)

There were 693 amateurs and eight professionals in the pro-am. This is open snooker and the professionals have by no means an easy task with giving 25 start. I was not destined to win both competitions this year, for Doug Mountjoy, a previous winner, beat me 4-3. I was 2-1 ahead and the one frame was conceded as a matter of strategy. Doug was leading 64-8 and there were seven reds left, so I did not want him to get potting practice at that stage. He did not really need it, for he went 3-2 ahead and I had to make a break of 115 and clear the table in the process of drawing level. He took the decider 89-35, with a 47 clearance to the pink.

Despite that setback, which in all the circumstances was hardly surprising, my successes made a considerable impact. Joe Davis said after that fifth world title win that I looked invincible and that I had a commanding presence at the table that made me look even taller than my 5ft 11in.

Doug Mountjoy, in fact, went on to beat me 7-6 in the Benson and Hedges Masters final at the New London Theatre. He was a professional of only four months standing and his form caused speculation on whether he could play right through the qualify-ing stages and win the world title, as Alex Higgins had done in 1972.

In the Benson and Hedges I beat Rex Williams 4-1, then beat Graham Miles 5-2 in the semifinals. World amateur champion Mountjoy deserved his success, though I lost concentration a little. In the tenth frame, while potting the black and scattering the pack, a red dropped into the middle pocket and this gave Doug a chance to make the highest break of the tournament, an 88, leaving only the black standing.

I made a trip over to Ireland to play in a round robin tourna-ment with Alex Higgins, Graham Miles and Dennis Taylor at Leopardstown Race Club, under the Benson and Hedges flag. I beat Graham Miles 4-1 and in the fourth frame missed a brown while on 97. Next I beat Alex Higgins 4-1, even though I needed in the second four blacks, a snooker and all the colours to tie. I did it and Alex went in-off the re-spotted black. Dennis Taylor beat me 3-2 and had to play a one-frame decider with Alex Higgins to see who should be a finalist. Alex produced one of his electrifying breaks of 70 and went on to beat me 5-4. It was a match full of tension and I made a break of 90 to make it 4-3. The next frame lasted for forty-five minutes of tactical snooker, but Alex was naturally a popular winner. He collected £750, a magnificent cut glass trophy and the award for the best break, a 126 against Dennis Taylor.

Danger breeds best on too much confidence   Corneille

There was a record £17,000 in prize-money for the 1977 world professional championships, which were being staged at the Crucible Theatre, Sheffield, with Mike Watterson as promoter. Though Embassy were the sponsors, smoking was forbidden, as far as the audience were concerned. The first eight in the rankings, myself, Alex Higgins, Eddie Charlton, Fred Davis, Graham Miles, Rex Williams, Perrie Mans and John Spencer were joined by eight qualifiers from the seventeen-man qualify-ing tournament. I was dieting, being very careful with the drink and was about one stone lighter. I had decided that although I would not seek any bother, it would help if there was a bit of aggro, for it seemed to help to get my adrenalin flowing.

This was the fiftieth year of the world professional final, first held in May 1927, at Camkin's Rooms in John Bright Street, Birmingham. Joe Davis, said to have bought his cue, 'Old Faithful', for 7s 6d (37½p) at a church bazaar, was champion for twenty years.

Joe Davis actually bought the first world trophy and it is the same one we are still playing for in Sheffield. Moving to that city was logical after the success of the New London Theatre. There was comfort and elegance in this new style snooker in the round, with the performers surrounded by their audience.

Just before the final, things were going well for me. My brother Ron, who had completed an eight year apprenticeship in the manufacture of snooker tables, joined me in a business venture in March 1977, when we formed Ray Reardon Snooker Ltd, registered in Bristol for the sale and maintenance of tables. Ron is now in business on his own in Bristol and he still does a lot of work for my company.

I approached my title defence in Sheffield feeling confident that the world championship trophy was my own property and that no one was going to take it from me, which I suppose is understandable after being the holder for four years in succession. It was a golden title to me and I do not say that in the light of the £6,000 first prize. It was a matter of prestige.

In the first round I beat Patsy Fagan 13-7. My opponent in the quarter-finals was John Spencer, with whom I had recently opened an international agency to promote equipment, including a two-piece cue. I was using my trusty old cue and John settled for one of the two-piece variety that we were promoting. It was a pretty good advertisement, although one I could well have done without, for with that cue John took my title. In the final he beat Cliff Thorburn. One of the factors in this defeat was that I was too relaxed and the adrenalin was not flowing. Yet the main snag, I am sure, was the travelling. At the end of the previous year I had made another trip to Australia, where

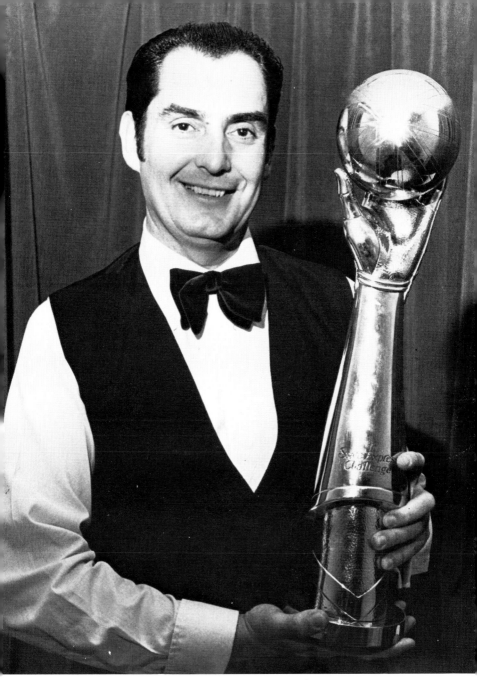

The first State Express world cup team championship was held in Birmingham in 1979. Terry Griffiths, Doug Mountjoy and myself joined forces and were proud to take the trophy for Wales. *Brian Marshall*

(*Above*) My boyhood efforts at learning to play the trumpet were never reinforced by natural talent, but I was still delighted to join in with the Audley Prize Band at a garden fete in Newcastle. (*Below*) My connection with Pontins holiday camps has been invaluable to my career as a professional snooker player, and I have enjoyed playing on their circuit for over thirteen years. Here Sir Fred Pontin keeps a close eye on the ball

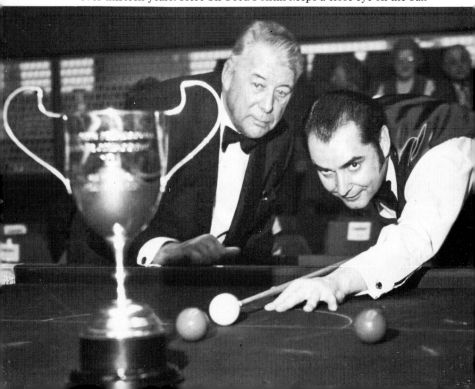

Eddie Charlton beat me in what was billed as the world match-play championship, but which did not have official blessing. Since then I had been constantly on the go. I was driving from one venue to another, staying in hotels, living out of a suitcase and giving exhibitions, so that it seemed to me at times that I was permanently on nights. In between exhibitions and tournaments I made a seven part instructional film, *Reardon on Snooker*, covering all aspects of the game, from tipping a cue to making a century break. It was first shown on Harlech Television in October 1977, and later on several other channels.

At least I got revenge over Doug Mountjoy, who had understandably said after beating me in the Benson and Hedges, 'I feel as if I have leaped to the top of a mountain at my first attempt.' It still left him a 33-1 outsider for the world championships. Anyway, in November I beat him in the William Hill professional snooker championship of Wales at Caerphilly. I was delighted to win this particular title, to say nothing of the £1,000 first prize. Doug got £500 as runner-up. This was another match with Doug Mountjoy that caused me embarrassment, not this time because I failed with the cue, but as a result of a lapse of memory. I discovered I had forgotten my dress suit and the start had to be delayed for thirty minutes while it was fetched from my Uncle Dan's house in Tredegar, which was still my headquarters when I played in Wales.

It was almost as if the gremlins were among those who attended the final, for a bulb in one of the television lights exploded and burned the table cloth so badly that it had to be replaced. Perhaps the lights were getting their own back for all the criticism I had hurled at them from time to time. On the second day of the final I awakened with a heavy cold, but still I won, for Doug Mountjoy's form was well below that which he had produced in the Benson and Hedges Masters. I think he was feeling jaded by all the travelling and the pressures he had encountered on turning professional.

That dress suit lapse was one of my very few in keeping thousands of engagements. I try to look my best on such occasions and generally I manage reasonably well, but there was one other occasion when I found myself in a real quandary. I ought to remember this one, for it made me one of the few people who have ever managed to take the shirt off the back of a bank manager.

I arrived to play at the Eccentric Club in Ryder Street, London, then discovered as I unpacked that I had not included a dress shirt. What was worse, the shops were shut and I could not think of any way in which I could beg, borrow or steal one. I wandered off down to the reception area, wondering what to do and hoping vaguely that I could enlist the help of a porter or someone else who could solve my problem. This is when I came across a bank manager named Bruce Stevans, who comes from Melbourne and with whom I had become friendly during one of my visits to Australia. He was on a visit to London and in the club he happened to spot a notice saying that I was playing there that night. He also learned that it was a dinner jacket only affair, so he went straight out and hired the appropriate outfit.

As we greeted each other, he must have been surprised by the enthusiasm I showed, until I said: 'Am I glad to see you. Can you lend me a dress shirt?' I explained my predicament and he grumbled a bit, saying he had only just collected the one he had hired. But do not let anyone tell you that all bank managers have hearts of stone. Bruce Stevans handed over his dress shirt, which fitted quite well, even if he is not as tall as I am. I looked as normal as I ever do and he got by dressed in a plain white shirt, under his suit, of course, so we all lived happily ever after. I owe him one, though. Not all bank managers would come up with a loan like that, even though Bruce said he was quite satisfied with the interest he got in watching the exhibition.

There was another embarrassing moment on the snooker scene. I was playing one morning at a Pontins camp and just when I bent over the table a woman holiday-maker put me off my stroke more than any opponent has been able to do. She piped up, 'Excuse me Mr Reardon, do you know you are wearing odd socks?' I found I had a brown sock on one foot and a grey sock on the other. I am never very bright first thing in the morning, but I had never made a mistake like that before, or at least, if I had, no one had seen fit to tell me so. The snag was that I could not blame anyone else. When I am away from home I always wash my own socks and smalls. I do not mind the chore and it saves me toting dirty washing around. Anyway, you can bet your life that since that day I have always checked my socks before leaving to play in public. It is not the sort of exhibition I wish to make of myself.

A circus is a place where animals are permitted to see people acting the fool Ambrose Bierce

About the time my television instructional film was being completed I was preparing for a trip to Canada, for the national exhibition championships in Toronto, which had been established in 1974. In previous years the tournament had been held in a permanent building, but this time the whole place had been booked by someone else, so a huge circus marquee was erected in the grounds to accommodate three snooker tables and seating for 1,000 spectators. Fittingly enough there was a traditional circus next door.

One way or another, the situation was not ideal. I do not know whether anyone has ever come up with the idea of a snooker circus, but if anyone does they can count me out. It was summer in Toronto and humid, so that the temperature inside the marquee was 100° F and there was a plague of pesky flies. The blue and white interior of the tent looked quite attractive, but it was not much good as a background against which the players could sight their shots, especially in the afternoons, when the arena was bathed in sunshine.

It was not sunny all the time. On one occasion there was a tremendous downpour of rain, which found some weak spots in the big top. I had a bit of fun by sheltering under a large umbrella, which I still have as a souvenir. The rainwater drained down the slope and under the tent, but we were standing on duckboards and did not get our feet wet. Mind you, it was the first time I made a bridge with my hand over a river.

In adjacent tents there was a steel band and also a non-stop dance band. What is more, the top turn in the circus was a dancing elephant and that is no silent routine, I can tell you. It did not stop our MC from making the funniest appeal of the tournament, asking spectators to be very quiet 'because the least distraction can upset the players'.

The previous year in this tournament, the balls had tended to jump out of the middle pockets and this problem had not been solved. Not many shots succeeded, partly because of conditions in the tent and partly because the table slate was only an inch thick and the cue ball tended to throw-off.

I lost in the semifinal to Alex Higgins, the eventual winner. I was no 3 seed behind John Spencer and Cliff Thorburn and, even less believable, Alex Higgins was no 5. I started with a 9-6 victory over eighteen years old Kirk Stevens of Scarborough, who at one time led 5-3, then I beat Stan Holden of Ontario, formerly of Bolton, 9-2. This brought me up against Alex Higgins, who forged 8-3 ahead and should have taken the twelfth game and the match, but missed the pink and allowed me to make it 8-4. I took advantage of that reprieve to haul him back to 8-7, but throughout the semifinal I was misjudging shots into the middle pocket on one side of the table and I did it fatally with the pink, leaving Alex a straight pot and all the remaining colours on their spots. He mopped up and took the frame and the match, 9-7.

This meant a repeat of the previous year's final, in which John Spencer beat Alex Higgins. John was finding conditions trying this time. He said: 'I chalked my cue once and the block of chalk broke in half. It was so hot it had got wet through in my pocket.' Perhaps it was the heat that caused a fairly considerable disagreement between the two in the final, but it did not stop Alex Higgins getting his revenge with some remarkable shots that had Joe Davis shaking his head in amazement. John Spencer missed a simple brown off its spot in the last frame and went down 17-14.

There were eighty-eight entrants in the open tournament and the top eight seeds, who also included Dennis Taylor, John

Pulman, Doug Mountjoy and Willie Thorne, started in the fourth round. Not many of them had encountered such conditions before and not many have since.

An hour of pain is as long as a day of pleasure   English Proverb

I was off across the Atlantic again in March 1978, for a twelve day visit to Trinidad to play in a pro-am golf tournament. I was going with my friend Roy Neale, who is a better than average golfer, is pretty handy at quite a number of other games and above all is a good companion, which is probably why I was in high spirits, with the prospect of some fun and relaxation before the world championships.

There are always pitfalls for the unwary and I found one while larking about with my son Darren, as we left the Midland Snooker Centre in the middle of Hanley. I slipped on the stairs and sprained my ankle rather badly. I was able to get to my car and to drive to Roy's house in Birmingham, because my car was an automatic. Roy drove us down to Heathrow the night before we were due to fly to Trinidad. We stayed overnight at a hotel and the next morning Roy knocked on my door and told me to get cracking. I had slept well, as I always do, but when I tried to get out of bed I found I could not walk.

I crawled to the door on my hands and knees and opened it, whereupon Roy immediately thought I was clowning and started to try to kick me to my feet. When he heard what I called him he stopped, had a look at my ankle and sent a porter out to buy me a walking stick, which I still possess. I managed to limp about a bit with the aid of that stick, but there was no way in which we were going to catch our plane. Roy pulled all kinds of strings to get us another flight the next day on the Dutch airline, KLM, whose stewards were simply great. They put me in a wheelchair and pushed me to the head of the queue. I have never had such preferential treatment, but there must be nicer ways of getting fussed over by the girls.

We were forced to take an incredibly roundabout route to Trinidad that I cannot remember in detail now, but it was 5 am when we landed. We were not surprised that there was no one to greet us. All we had was a phone number. We left it a couple of hours for the sake of decency, for we reckoned that if we rang someone at 5 am to say, 'We're here,' they just might tell us where to go next and it was hot enough in Trinidad. Around 7 am we began dialling the Victoria Golf Club and though the number rang and rang, no one answered.

Eventually we gave it up as a bad job, found a hotel, had some breakfast and a couple of hours of sleep. Then we started to phone again and still there was no reply, which puzzled us, for this was the day on which the pro-am was due to start. In the end we had to take a taxi the twenty or so miles to the course and when we arrived things were getting into full swing. They greeted us warmly and inquired where we had been, so we had to take deep breaths before asking why the hell they did not answer the phone. 'Never rung, been here all the time,' we were told. It turned out that the number we had been ringing, the one that was still listed, was that at the old course. This was a new course and they had a new number.

We told them the old number had been ringing out and they tried it too. Sure enough, it rang out. That was a real mystery, for there was by now a housing estate on what had been the old golf course. Somewhere in the middle of it a ghost phone was ringing unanswered. At least they found out for themselves that what we had said was so, which prevented them from blaming our story on a combination of heat, drink and national lunacy.

My ankle would not allow me to take part in the pro-am, but there was no escape for Roy, who soon found himself perspiring in a hundred degrees of heat as he literally steamed his way round the golf course. During the two and half hours of that tournament he aged visibly, while I tried hard to rest in a manner of which I am sure my doctor would have approved. Roy, of course, is not medically trained, which probably explains why his face did not register approval when he tottered into sight and saw me lying by the pool, with my feet dangling in the cool water. I flopped into the pool and surfaced without damaging the Caribbean lager I was supping, but that did not seem to cheer him up, either. In fact I thought I detected a look of despair on his face.

I did not spend all my time lounging by the pool, for I was able to take in a few games of snooker in preparation for the fast approaching world championship.

A mutual sense of fun cements my friendship with Roy and it has been known to lead us into some pretty crazy situations. There was a typical example one night when we were in a Chinese restaurant in Trinidad. When I put down the pepper-pot, Roy promptly moved up the salt and said, 'Checkmate.' It started a completely unpremeditated game of mock chess, using the condiments and other items on the table. We pondered the moves with care and this attracted the attention of a waiter.

Soon that waiter was pointing out to a colleague our strange behaviour. That made us worse and we began to register annoyance and delight, even paying out and starting another game. By now the Chinese staff were thoroughly interested, for any form of gambling attracts them as moths to a lamp. When our waiter started to ask questions we brushed him aside as we concentrated and when he tried to take away an empty glass we shouted at him, warning him to leave it alone and that he might have cost me a lot of money.

Eventually, of course, we had to get on with our meal and in any case we could not keep our faces straight any longer. We told them that this was a famous old British game, something like chess in its origins. The Chinese staff, even those from the kitchen. were fascinated by now and begged us to explain the rules, even offering to bet on the outcome if we would play one more game. We said we had not got enough time and had to eat before we left. They offered us money to explain the game, but we apologised and said we would do so when we next visited the restaurant. We were flying home the next day, so they must still be waiting for details, unless of course they have realised that the British can be inscrutable sometimes, too.

11

GIN AND TONIC VICTORY

Drunkenness lifts the burden from anxious minds
Horace (Epistles)

On my return in early April my ankle was still a bit troublesome and I needed to hone my form for the world championship in Sheffield, where at the Crucible Theatre I beat Doug Mountjoy 13-9 and Bill Werbeniuk 13-6. That took me to the semifinals and another clash with Eddie Charlton. Once more things did not go too well for me at the start, especially when my concentration was disturbed by television commentator Ted Lowe, but I made the effort and ended the day two frames ahead. Things were looking good.

I was staying at the luxurious home of my friend Gordon Ingham at South Owram, Halifax

During the championships it was my routine to get up early for a twenty minute swim in his pool, followed by half an hour of practice on the snooker table, then a light breakfast and a morale boosting drive to Sheffield in Gordon's Rolls-Royce. There is nothing quite like arriving in a Rolls to make you feel like an aristocrat and, apart from that, when I reached the Crucible Theatre on the second day of the semifinal I felt marvellous, mentally and physically. In fact, I had never felt better and I was ready to climb mountains, jump rivers and pot the lot blindfold.

Do not ask me why things went so wrong, because I do not know. I cannot explain why it was that I was unable to pot a ball and lost 6-1. Nothing went in and to say that I was fed up would be the understatement of the year. When I got back into the Rolls for the return trip to South Owram I could not have felt more miserable if I had been heading for a funeral, so I said to Gordon Ingham: 'Book us in for dinner tonight and we will have a right booze-up. We will take our wives and your daughter and have a real night out.'

Gordon immediately registered concern and started to reason with me, pointing out that I was only five frames adrift and telling me in no uncertain terms that I was taking a very silly attitude. When I insisted he told me I was mad, but I said I was going out with or without them so they fell in with my wishes. We booked a table, had a couple of large gin and tonics in the lounge and set off for the restaurant in Leeds. There we started with two more large gin and tonics and followed them at the table with two bottles of red wine, two bottles of white wine, some brandies and a bottle of champagne. We proceeded to get really smashed, then returned to South Owram, where we had a couple more large gin and tonics before staggering off to bed around 4 am.

Someone got me up at 7.30 am for my swim and watched I did not drown, either by accident or choice. I managed a very light breakfast and felt the old truth about hangovers, that at first you are afraid you are going to die, then you are afraid that you won't. We drove to Sheffield in a merciful silence and when I walked out to resume my semifinal I felt truly dreadful.

My eyes were not functioning properly, in fact, as the French say, they were not lined up with the holes in my skull. I had a thick head, hot flushes, the lot. I potted everything in sight and won 7-0.

Eddie Charlton and I were interviewed before the television cameras by David Vine, who quite naturally was wondering what was going on, why my form was fluctuating so wildly, likewise the state of my health. I told him my delicate condition was due to taking a few drinks the night before, though I did not tell him the whole truth and nothing but the truth, for I did not want to give everyone the impression I had suddenly become an alcoholic. Even so, I confessed to a binge big enough to cause a minor sensation, especially as I had won nine frames out of 11 to beat Eddie Charlton 18-14.

I cannot explain why I knew a night's boozing was the answer when I had felt so well and had played so badly. Perhaps it is that the tension is less when all you are conscious of is how awful you feel. It may be that when you know you are not functioning properly you take extra care with every shot. I do not know. I can only tell you that it worked, though it is not a remedy I would want to repeat too often. When you have got a sore head you do not have much inclination to wear even a world crown.

My opponent in the final was Perrie Mans, the first South African to reach the last two in the competition. Perrie had earned the nickname Billy Thud by the strength of his potting and he justified it by his display, which is remembered by the millions of television viewers for a fantastic shot that sank the pink. In the end though I beat him 25-18 to take the world championship for the sixth time in nine years.

I put the title beyond Perrie's grasp by taking three in a row in the last session: 82-43, with the help of a break of 81; 75-44, 60-49, with breaks of 36 and 35, respectively.

In August and September of that year I visited Tokyo, by the Polar route that knocks eight hours off the time from Britain to Japan, and also went to South Africa again. At home we had moved from the privacy and relative solitude of Shropshire to Werrington, that area on the edge of Stoke-on-Trent where we have always seemed to be happiest. We were back among our closest friends again and it helped Sue while I was away.

I won first prize of £2,000 in the Daily Mirror Champion of Champions tournament promoted by Mike Barrett at Wembley Conference Centre. In the semifinals I had an easy task in beating Patsy Fagan 6-1. (Frame scores: 108-1, 95-33, 109-14, 89-30, 74-47, 17-76, 77-48.) My opponent in the final was Alex Higgins, who usually plays well against me because he knows he has to be at his best.

Alex was not at his best in the first session. I played well, going into a 3-0 lead. I was trailing 40-0 in the second and cleared the table with a break of 90 and I came from behind to win the third. I was 4-1 ahead at the end of the session, then

Alex hauled me back to 5-4, even though I had a break of 70. I was 8-4 in front at the end of that session, then slipped from 9-5 to 9-9. It was a break of 77 in the nineteenth frame that decided it, for Alex was thoroughly disheartened. I won the final frame, too. (Frame scores: 125-8, 90-43, 75-46, 28-108, 60-43, 20-114, 13-101, 104-19, 1-140, 84-22, 78-36, 101-18, 12-100, 73-48, 41-90, 51-60, 23-83, 30-72, 78-46, 94-12.)

I beat Doug Mountjoy in the 1979 Pot Black final to become champion again ten years after my first success, but there were lean years ahead.

Years steal vigour from the limb   Byron

About this time I began to realise how top models must feel when the wrinkles begin to appear, with flecks of grey in the hair and unkind messages from the bathroom scales. My concern was not with the signs of wear and tear I could detect in myself in the bathroom mirror, but those in my faithful old cue that I won in a Joe Davis competition in 1957. It is a Burwat Champion, 4ft 8in long and slightly heavier than the average at 17½oz. It is handbuilt, with a butt made of five different pieces of black ebony. The cue is ash with a wide grain and the tip is 9.8 millimetres. It has had more tips than a head waiter.

What it has meant to me can be judged by my reaction when it was stolen in South Africa and returned; and even more by my lack of success in the past couple of years, which I attribute not to any faltering of my ability, or even to the rising standards of the opposition, but to problems with my cue.

I have made jokes to people saying, 'You can take out my wife, but not my cue,' and though I know no one would take that seriously, it does pair together the two priceless props of my career. It has been to me what Excalibur was to King Arthur, the magic sword given to the ancient British hero of the sixth century by the Lady of the Lake, to ensure his immunity to severe wounds and loss of blood. Joe Davis was the snooker rock from whom I drew it and it has served me as faithfully and well as any friend.

After the 1971 mishap in Leeds I had no serious trouble until the summer of 1976 at Pontins Camp at Sands Bay, where I played a deep screw shot, heard a click of ominous proportions and found an inch and a half had broken off my cue. I had hit the shot hard, as required, but the white had not travelled far. I suppose I should have been embarrassed, with all those people watching, but I felt too numbed by the shock to register any other feeling. A fault had developed in my cue and I knew I was in trouble.

Rex Williams had a company who could deal with this kind of a problem and I consulted them. They fitted a new ferrule and added an inch and a half to the butt. This is a thin cue, so the business end was not much different when the job was done, but it still took me almost a year to get back to the pinpoint accuracy that is essential to the professional game.

Late in 1978 another two inches broke off the cue when the end split and I knew now that I really did have problems. I did not like the idea of having it glued together, for obviously it might go again at a critical moment.

In the ranks of the snooker fraternity in North Staffordshire I had met an engineer named Tony Wilshaw and this friend became not only my cue doctor, but a consultant for quite a number of top players, amateur and professional. We discussed my problem and it became evident that major surgery was required. Tony says it brought him out in a cold sweat when he thought about the operation. Can you imagine a blacksmith telling King Arthur, 'I am sorry, but I have ruined Excalibur.'

For Tony it was a bit like starting your career as a surgeon with a heart transplant, but he gritted his teeth, fitted a new ferrule, added four inches to the butt, then tapered down the cue in an effort to restore the balance. It meant cutting an inch and a half off one end and splicing on a similar length at the other end. This most delicate operation was carried out in a workshop at his home, for this was his hobby. His job was with a commercial repair firm in Fenton, the Potteries town that novelist Arnold Bennett forgot.

Tony did his work with loving care and it is a tribute to his ability that I was able to beat John Spencer in the Forward Chemicals tournament in Manchester; but the adjustments meant that the butt was getting longer, the shaft shorter and the cue was getting solid and was creating a throw-off on the cue ball.

That is no reflection on Tony, who says his work for me resembled a Royal appointment. One of his jobs was to make eight splices in rebuilding a cue for Alex Higgins and he went on to make a break of 135 with it in the Coral UK pool competition. Cliff Wilson also became a customer. Tony had to have his garage extended to cope with the work, which at times has threatened to overwhelm his normal occupation. It takes two weeks of solid work to rebuild a cue and being an engineer enabled Tony to make his own set of unique tools for the job. He has been kind enough to say that he learned a great deal of what he knows about cues from me.

As far as my cue was concerned though, I began to think that the problem was terminal and the full cure beyond him or anyone else. I was making allowance for the throw-off and I was just unable to play consistent top class snooker. After the 1981 championships I knew it was time for a decision. We talked it over and decided on a kill-or-cure operation. Tony would take two inches off the cue and add two inches to the butt, then taper down the finished article. I knew the likelihood and cost of failure. Tony carried out the operation in late April, then returned the cue to me. It was a strange cue as far as playing was concerned, totally unfamiliar. It is no exaggeration to say that I felt as if I had been bereaved.

The new always carries with it the sense of sacrilege
Henry Miller

Some years ago I began collecting old cues of a type similar to mine and I suppose that without realising my motive I may have been seeking a replacement. If that is so I was unsuccessful until early in 1981 when my friend Roy Neale visited my home one day to play me in a practice session and said, 'Why

139

don't you try my cue?' As a friend he knew my problems.

This cue is about 70 years old and it once belonged to his father. It is a Peall Record Cue, with an 11 mm tip, which is a bit wider than my Burwat Champion. With it, less than two months after I had said my requiem for the old cue, I made a maximum break in Perth, Scotland. It was my thirteenth maximum and I regarded it as anything but unlucky, for I thought my problems were solved.

It was not to be so and after more setbacks and a particularly frustrating defeat in Scotland, I spoke a bit rashly in public about retiring. I was not serious, but the story hit the headlines and I had offers of cues from all over Britain and from as far afield as Johannesburg.

It became clear to me that the old cue was impossible to replace and I decided to have one more go at putting things right. My friends Herman Bond and David Webb at the St Mellion Golf and Country Club in Saltash, Cornwall, put me in touch with the headmaster of the nearby Callington Comprehensive School, Mr Neville Nortop. He let me call upon the services of the head of the woodwork department, Mr Arthur Fleetwood, and his senior assistant, Mr Tony Speare.

They took the cue to pieces three times in three days. We found that the lead used to weight the cue was much too far up the shaft and it had to be drilled out. I could feel the improvement and made a break of 141 during a show, but it was still not right and there had to be more drilling. I tried it again at a show on my 49th birthday and made three century breaks, 105, 119 and 120. Now I can pot the long balls again and the psychological problems seem to be going, so that I look forward again to practice and to competition.

I have always been surprised by the amount of material wasted by cue manufacturers, especially since a lot of it is ebony and that is not exactly cheap. The standard cue is 4ft 10in long and most people hold the butt about a couple of inches from the end. My old cue is 4ft 8in long and at a very early stage I realised that most of the top players did not use a cue of standard length.

Alex Higgins has one of the shortest, about 4ft 7in. I have told people in the trade about the waste in manufacturing cues to 4ft 10in, but no one has ever paid any heed.

For what do we live, but to make sport for our neighbours
Jane Austen

March of 1979 brought me an award won only once before, by Derek Randall, the Nottinghamshire and England cricketer. In a ballot of the Home Counties, conducted by the now unhappily defunct *London Evening News*, I was voted Most Entertaining Personality of the Year. The event was run in conjunction with Concert Artists of Great Britain, whose president, Bill Pertwee, presented the award to me at a ball organised specially for the purpose.

In June of that year I was one of four sportsmen to be presented with an illuminated address and a gold medal by the Sports Council of Wales. It was a great honour to be in the company of Great Britain show jumping star David Broome, Gareth Evans, the prince of Rugby Union, and the then British 110 metres hurdles champion, Berwyn Price.

People who are masters in their own house are never tyrants
Napoleon

A couple of months later, amid growing tensions, we seemed to be on the verge of a breakaway in snooker of the kind Kerry Packer masterminded in cricket. Professional snooker is very fortunate, in that it has only become a major force in recent years. I know Joe Davis was world champion from 1927 to 1946, but the take-off did not really begin until the late 1960s. Consequently snooker is a rarity among sports; one run very largely by the players, as distinct from the many that are organised by amateur officials who, over the years, have developed their own aristocracy. Player power, though, does not mean harmony. There are times when I wish we could all agree about something.

After the 1979 world championship, won by fellow Welshman Terry Griffiths, the World Professional Billiards and Snooker Association met at a Sheffield hotel for about ten hours and it almost ended with a split in the ranks. The row was over world championship rules and a change forced through by the more numerous, but less successful players. Under the old rule the top eight in the ranking list did not have to take part in the qualifying stages and this meant that a place in the finals before the television cameras was assured. Players are well aware that this is of benefit even to those who do not win. The new rule exempted only the champion and runner-up from the qualifying stages, which meant there were fourteen places available, instead of eight, which is why it commanded a majority vote.

I was among those who thought this was a classic case of the tail wagging the dog and it led to the founding of the Professional Snooker Association Ltd, in which I played a leading role. We felt the new organisation would do a much better job of negotiating with the television companies, promoters and sponsors, for snooker's progress in that direction still left a lot to be desired. We were aware that, if necessary, the new body could become the alternative governing body in the sport, in the same way that the World Boxing Council and the World Boxing Association operate.

There were months of argument, but in the end the breakaway was avoided and I belive that was a good thing. It was agreed to amend the constitution of the World Professional Billiards and Snooker Association, so that the top ten in the ranking list automatically form the committee. I was elected chairman, which was another responsibility to carry, in addition to fending off the increasing challenge from the new talent in the ranks of professional snooker.

It is common sense that the top ten professionals make the vital decisions, but there was a compromise. As before, the top eight in the rankings were exempted from the world championship qualifying competition, but the number to play in the finals at Sheffield was increased from sixteen to twenty-four. Numbers nine to sixteen automatically went for-

At home with some of my trophies

(*Above*) The real Pot Black trophy. The BBC television series had a tremendous impact on the public and did much to boost the popularity of snooker. (*Below*) In Perth, Scotland, summer 1981, at the home of Raymond Clive Miquel, who challenged me to a golf-tennis-snooker triathlon. He lost – but not before trouncing me on the tennis court

ward to the first round at the Crucible Theatre, Sheffield, and the remaining eight players, as before, had to win a place in the qualifiers.

Where personal interests, money and professional status are concerned, feelings can run pretty high and the arguments took on some of the worst aspects of a family feud before common sense prevailed. It was just as well that agreement was reached, for the sponsors and television people were getting pretty fed up with it in the end. Happily that is all in the past and at least we have this safeguard: that no one can be keener than the top ten players to preserve the success and prosperity of the sport.

Fortune brings in some boats that are not steered   Shakespeare

Since the days of the Gutless Wonder I have driven upwards of half a million miles in this country and abroad, without injuring myself or anyone else, but there have been one or two hairy moments. At home the worst one was in October 1979, when damage that cost £9,000 to put right was done to the Rolls-Royce I was driving.

It was a Silver Shadow belonging to Gordon Ingham, of Halifax, who with his wife was a passenger. I was driving the three of us back from the State Express World Snooker Cup event in Birmingham. It was around midnight and we were travelling north on the M6 between the Stafford and Stone turn-offs and were in the slow lane, doing about 65 mph. Ahead I saw a light flashing and moved out into the middle lane, since the problem seemed to be dead ahead of me. In fact a truck and a car had been in collision.

There was a car in the fast lane and we were creeping up on him when we moved into the middle lane. I think the driver must have fallen asleep, for suddenly he went straight into the barrier and bounced back into the Rolls I was driving. I was watching him carefully and anticipated what was happening by pulling to my left to ride the blow, but his car bounced back

145

against the barrier, then rebounded into us once more. Again I managed to ride the impact, then I pulled up on the hard shoulder. He stopped 100 yards or so further on and instinctively I realised that he was going to drive away.

My police training took charge and I got out of the car and ran up the hard shoulder. The car that had collided with us was driven away, but not before I had noted the number. By this time the police were arriving to attend the accident between the other car and the truck, so that I informed them about what had happened to us and they stopped the vehicle that had damaged the Rolls before it had been driven for more than five minutes or so from the scene. I think the other driver panicked and I understand that later he was dealt with by the courts. Gordon and his wife were convinced that it was only the strength of the stressed steel monocoque body of the Rolls that saved us from at least serious injury, but that is not my opinion. Mind you, our car would have been much more badly damaged had it not been so strong.

While I am on the subject of accidents on the roads, let me tell you about a couple in South Africa, the country where I think driving conditions are the worst in the world. For instance, people are allowed to pass you on the nearside and on occasions they take horrific risks.

There was one occasion when we were taking Jimmy van Rensburg to the airport to catch his plane to Rhodesia and a lorry travelling in the opposite direction shot straight across in front of us. He only missed us because I banged our car into second gear and it checked us just enough. The lorry went off the road and rolled over and over, finishing on its roof. I ran to it and could not open the damaged door, but I managed to get the rear door of the vehicle open and found myself staring into the eyes of the driver, who was hanging upside down. He was not hurt and we managed to get him out, but what shook me was that he showed no reaction at all to the escape we had all just experienced. There was no sign of fear or anything else. Like a lot of African drivers, I think that when he got behind the wheel he thought he was Fangio, or someone like that famous driver.

There was an even worse incident when brother Ron was a passenger. I was driving down a very steep hill and the road was wet. There had been an accident on a bend and people were actually standing in the middle of the road.

By the time I got on to the bend and saw them, I knew I was in trouble. I said to Ron, 'Hold on, we are going to spin.' I knew that would happen in those road conditions when I braked and we did spin, but fortunately we stopped with the rear wheels on the rim of a ravine.

In my early days on the Pontins circuit I had an escape that frightened me to pieces. I was driving a Zephyr Six down the A12 from Lowestoft to Camber, Rye, and was travelling at 70 mph in the fast lane when the bonnet flew open and produced a tremendous bang as it welded itself across the roof of the car, completely obscuring my vision. I tried to remember where the nearest vehicles were as I slowed down and filtered across to the side of the road, remarkably without being hit. When I pulled the bonnet down it overlapped the front of the car by a foot. I managed to secure it with wire and complete my journey. In fact I used the car for the rest of the week, when I was able to get the bonnet replaced.

I also had problems when driving one winter from Hereford to Abergavenny, going very slowly because there was slush on the road. Suddenly I started to slide and went straight off the road. I saw the stump of a tree in the field and said to myself, 'I am going to hit that,' which I did. The car was a write-off, but I was unhurt.

My last mishap occurred in September 1981, in a narrow country lane in Devon. I came upon a tractor towing a farm implement and sensed trouble. I stopped the car, unfastened my seat belt and threw myself on the floor, which was just as well, for the implement tilted over and scalped my car. I might have had an unscheduled haircut.

I have always enjoyed driving the Gordon Ingham Rolls-Royce, though I do not have one of my own and have no ambitions in that direction. However, I do have to confess to one form of one-upmanship, for since 1974 I have had my personal numberplate, 1 PRO, which is currently fitted on my Royale. The first few numbers in the PRO series belonged to British Rail at Stoke and I am given to understand that 1 PRO was fitted to the station master's van.

My brother-in-law, Ron Carter, formerly well known as a cyclist with Burslem Olympic Wheelers and as a Formula II racing driver, paid a call at Hartshill Motors in Stoke-on-Trent in the course of his second-hand car business inquiries. He was looking through a pile of logbooks when he spotted the 1 PRO numberplate and said, 'I know someone who will buy this vehicle.' I paid £500 for it the next day, leaving the van to be scrapped. I reckon the numberplate is worth a few bob now. I do not know what happened to numbers 2, 3 and 4 PRO, all of which I believe were with British Rail at Stoke, but I am glad Sue's brother was quick to realise the value of the one I possess.

To forget one's ancestors is to be a tree without a root
Chinese Proverb

When I went to Dublin in 1974 to play Gary Owen I learned something about the family tree that surprised me, for I had supposed that we had always belonged to the Welsh valleys.

Not so, I was told. The name Reardon is a derivative of Riorden, from County Cork, which apparently must have been home to some of my ancestors. As a result of this visit to Dublin I have on the wall of the lounge at home in Werrington a family coat of arms, given to me as a souvenir of the visit. The Latin motto is *Pro Deo et Patria,* which being translated means, 'For God and Country'. The crest is a *fleur-de-lis gules,* or heraldic lily on a red background. The Blazon of Arms says:

'Quarterly – 1st and 4th gules out of clouds, in the sinister side a dexter arm fessways proper, holding a dagger in pale argent, pommel and hilt or; 2nd and 3rd, argent, a lion rampant gules against a tree in the dexter couped proper.'

You will gather that the main features are an arm holding a dagger that has a pale silver pommel and a gold hilt, plus a lion rampant, or erect. I do not know what my ancestors did to warrant those symbols, but they obviously did not encourage people to take liberties.

If I were to have a new coat of arms created, using modern symbols, I suppose there would be incorporated the Red Dragon of Wales; a bottle oven to represent the Potteries, perhaps with the Staffordshire Knot; a miner's helmet or a pick to mark my years in the coal industry; a policeman's helmet or possibly handcuffs to commemorate my years in uniform; and, of course, dominating them all a snooker cue.

I might even insist that there be a warning sign, though one more subtle than a dagger, for I do not take any more kindly than did my ancestors to people who try to take advantage of good nature.

12
SHOW BIZ VENTURES

Everything is funny, as long as it's happening to somebody else
Will Rogers

There have been occasions when I have taken liberties and one of them was when I was a guest on the *Parkinson Show* on television in January 1979. The interview itself went more or less to plan, but I surprised Michael Parkinson in the second part of the show by telling a joke that he did not expect.

It was the story of the company director, whose new secretary had curves in all the right places. She had been working for him for only a few weeks when they had one of those days when there is hardly time to breathe. They managed to snatch only a cup of coffee and a sandwich during the day, so when the grateful boss gave her a lift home the secretary invited him in for a drink. As they relaxed they realised they were hungry and the secretary offered to rustle up a meal. The boss nipped across to the off-licence while she was getting the food ready and came back with a bottle of wine, which made them seem even more attractive to one another, so that they finished up in bed. Inevitably they dozed off to sleep and it was very late when the boss awoke and realised he would have to dash off home. He said to his secretary: 'Before I go, rub some of that whisky into my hair and dust me down a bit with this billiard chalk.'

When he got home his angry wife demanded an explanation and he said to her: 'I ran my new secretary home and we had food and some wine and finished up in bed.' His wife said: 'Don't tell lies to me. You reek of whisky and you are covered in chalk. You have been with your damned mates playing snooker in the club again.'

I also played a few tricks on Michael Parkinson that night. When it was trick shot time Michael wanted to have a go and I managed to arrange the cues in the rack with the butts crossed, so that when he tried to pull his cue from the rack with the usual flourish, he pulled the lot over. We went through the repertoire and he wanted to finish with the tricks involving a wicker bottle, potting the balls in through the narrow neck, then the one when the red goes in and chases out the white. The wicker bottle was placed by the side of the table on the floor, in readiness. At the appropriate time I sidled round to the bottle and kicked it right under the table. When Michael reached down for it he found he had to crawl about on his hands and knees.

It was quite hilarious and I think Michael Parkinson got as much fun out of the show as I did. Certainly a lot of viewers indicated that they did, even from some very unexpected quarters. After the show the producer, John Fisher, rang my wife, Sue, and said they had received a message from Buckingham Palace saying how much the show had been enjoyed. I do not think the producer was pulling my leg, but you never know what reprisals to expect if you play tricks on people.

There is an ambush everywhere from the army of accidents   Hafiz

There are occasions when trick shots can go wrong, but usually it is just a hiccup, a matter of trying again and succeeding at the second attempt, or at worst the third. One night at Plymouth about four years ago provided the exception and it happened after I had finished my stint and someone in the audience requested the whisky bottle shot. If he was a friend, I did not need an enemy that night.

The trick involves placing a ball on top of a full bottle of whisky and another on the table, about six or eight inches away from the bottle. You then make the cue ball strike the one on the table, then jump up to knock the ball off the top of the bottle. Obviously there is room for error, so it is better to use a round bottle, for that is less likely to break if it is knocked down.

Manager Bill Oliver either did not hear me properly or did

151

not understand what I said to him, for when he went to fetch the whisky from his stock he came back with that brand in a triangular-shaped bottle. With the advantage of hindsight I know I should have insisted on a round bottle, even if it kept the crowd waiting, for I did not get the shot quite right and the cue ball took a trajectory that was about two inches too low. It struck the neck of the bottle and sent it crashing down. Sure enough the bottle broke and the whisky flooded the table.

The shock caused a silence you could feel, until I broke the tension with a rather hysterical laugh. That opened the floodgates and everybody fell about, so that the place was in an uproar. Club officials were more anxious than amused and they rushed forward with towels to mop the table, but I knew this would take out the dye, so I stopped them and called for a bucket of water. I threw the water all over the table, on the basis that it would dilute the whisky. That was my last trick of the night and the crowd went home to remember my misfortune longer than my skill. I told the manager to let the table dry and said I would ring him a couple of days later to see if the cloth needed replacing. When I did inquire I was told the cloth was not quite as green as it had been, but it would be all right and I did not need to replace it with a new one. I was glad about that, for it saved me between £150 and £200.

Still, it is not every day you down a whole bottle of scotch in one go and only dilute it afterwards. Not a trick to repeat, that one.

Over the bottle many a good friend is found   Yiddish Proverb

I have happier associations with whisky and especially with the Bell's Scotch Whisky Company and their remarkable chairman and managing director, Raymond Clive Miquel.

My links with Bell's started in 1976, when I took part in exhibition games in Leeds, Stoke, Swansea and Birmingham that raised around £6,000 for licensed trade charities. In Stoke I met the best woman player I have ever encountered, Ann

Johnson of Cheltenham. John Dunning and Fred Davis also took part.

We had a similar series in 1978 and again in 1980, when we played in Birmingham, Derby, Swansea and Slough. Terry Griffiths, Steve Davis, the present world champion, and Graham Miles have all joined in and over the three years in which we played I think something like £20,000 was raised.

This had two sequels. One was that I was presented with an engraved silver bell, the symbol of the company, for the help given since 1976. The other was that I was invited to the home of Raymond Clive Miquel in June 1981, to face him in a triathlon competition. I reckon the Bell's chief was tired of losing to me at snooker and decided to take me on at golf and tennis as well. At least it gave him a very sporting chance, for oddly enough I had never played tennis before and found out next day that I had muscles I had never even suspected.

It was a magnificent weekend and I could not have lived better if I had been blessed with the wealth of Onassis. I was thoroughly beaten on the courts at the Perth Tennis Club, but won the other two, clinching my victory on the golf course. However, it was the snooker that mattered most, as I have related. I was using my new cue from Roy Neale, and with it on the 13th of the month I made the thirteenth maximum break of 147 of my career and my 3,049th century break. One of my souvenirs of that weekend is a golf putter, with the business end shaped like a bottle of Bell's, though with one surface flat, so that it could be used for putting. Whenever I look at it, I shall not be thinking about golf.

Over the years I have played in a lot of pro-am golf and pro-celebrity golf and one of the happiest occasions of this kind was in Scotland at Gleneagles, where I was paired with Lee Trevino. The Super Mex is just that, a fantastic man, who was even better than I expected him to be. He was pleasant and considerate, joking despite some dreadful weather and being pestered by an army of admirers. He even found time to show me some trick shots and I shall remember him as a lovely man it was a pleasure to meet.

153

I have always enjoyed my visits to Scotland. I was the first professional snooker player to tour there, largely through Riley Burwat general manager Bob Baillee, who has done so much for the game in Scotland. In October 1977, he even had me flying off to play an exhibition game for the oil workers at the Sullom Voe terminal in the Shetlands. I hoped I helped to brighten that bleak place for a while.

Bob Baillee figured in an amusing story involving a Glasgow policeman. We were driving home one night when he had enjoyed himself and I had stayed cold sober. We were signalled to stop by a police car, so I told him to stay where he was and I got out. As a result of questioning me the policeman realised who I was and asked me for my autograph, but when Bob saw him pulling out his notebook for this purpose he thought I was being booked. He got out of the car with difficulty and did my cause no good at all.

Another amusing incident in London a few years ago involved a police officer, though this time he was a CID man who was with his wife in a party that also included Gordon Ingham. After dinner we decided to go on to a club and our CID friend said he would get a taxi. What we did not know was he was going to get an authentic London cab that was used by the CID when keeping observations on someone. He drove it himself and when we got in Gordon did not recognise him. It was only when we got to the other end and he tried to pay the driver and give him a tip that he suddenly realised that he knew the cabbie.

One of my most recent trips to Scotland was for the opening of a club that bears my name, Reardon's Snooker Centre, at 177 Trongate, Glasgow. I was consulted throughout about the layout, type and position of table, lighting, decor, acoustics, equipment and furniture. There are twenty-eight tables, four of them to championship specification in private rooms. There is a membership fee of £17.50 and the table charge is £2 an hour to members and guests only. It is one of the finest private snooker clubs of its kind in the country.

In our play we reveal what kind of people we are   Ovid

One of the best kept secrets in golf concerns The World's Greatest Golfers Association, of which I am chairman, with a full vote. Brixham bank official Mike Gilbert is vice-chairman, with full vote, and secretary David Webb is both non-voting and unpaid. The headquarters are at Churston and there is a Perpetual Trophy that is insured against fire, flood, theft, third party claims, acts of God and woodworm. In the revised rules the aims and objects include providing Messrs Reardon and Gilbert, hereinafter referred to as the winners, with a constant supply of golf balls. There are highly detailed rules, which are vested in the sub-commitee comprising Messrs Gilbert, Reardon and Webb, whose term of office does not expire until the last day of this century and who need not at all times be impartial. All of which adds up to the fact that when I am in the South West during the summer, golf at Churston and the company there rank high among my more pleasurable activities.

Happily I am one of those people who get pleasure out of most things on most days. There is even enjoyment in appearing on television and radio shows that have nothing to do with snooker, despite the fact that those of us who are professionals in sport are amateurs in that line of business. I have appeared in the *Generation Game*, the *Paul Daniel's Magic Show*, the *Little and Large Show*, the *Russ Abbot Show*, *Punch Lines*, *A Question of Sport* and with Arthur Negus talking about antiques.

We have got a lot of the television shows I have done recorded on video cassettes, but the main radio show caused problems. When I was on *Desert Island Discs*, a power cut in our area upset Sue's plans to record it and she had to sit and listen on the car radio until she saw lights go on in neighbouring houses. Then she rushed in to record the last minutes.

I often wonder what impression we create in the minds of the public. Let me tell you two stories about John Pulman.

There was an occasion when an opponent who shall be nameless played wild shots on three successive visits to the table and each time left the cue ball safe.

Those of us who were watching saw John Pulman register disbelief on his face the first time, mounting frustration that he disclosed with a couple of earthy asides on the second occasion, then came the third. We expected an explosion when John went to the table and found that once again a hit-and-miss shot had left him precisely nothing. He stared at the table and we waited with bated breath. Finally, John said, 'Do you think he played that?' It broke the tension.

On another occasion John was playing against me and he made a fractional error that left the blue in the jaws of the pocket, which he knew would cost him the match. After he had played the shot he just stood there, anger mounting in his face. I thought, 'I am keeping out of that,' but John still did not move and eventually I had to give way. I walked to the table, fearing the worst, but John just looked me straight in the eye and said, 'Say thank you.' I said, 'Thank you,' and he just walked away. Those are classic examples by John Pulman on how to master your temperament. A lot of people in other sports could learn by watching John.

People ask me about that tough Aussie, Eddie Charlton, who before he became a world-class snooker player proved his all-round ability at other sports, including boxing. Eddie is, like all Aussies, fiercely competitive, but he is not an aggressive man away from the table. Though he rarely smiles, he has a very good tenor voice and can sing a ballad well enough to bring tears to your eyes.

I remember that after I had beaten him in Manchester in the 1975 final he was naturally dejected, but he soon shook off that mood. When I returned to the hotel about 2 am after celebrating with friends, Eddie was a lone figure in the lounge and he shouted me across to join him in a drink. There was no trace of bitterness or rancour. That is the kind of sportsman I admire.

Two players with whom I have been proud to represent Wales are Terry Griffiths and Doug Mountjoy. We won the first State Express World Cup team championship in 1979 in Birmingham and retained it in 1980 at the New London Theatre.

Younger players today are different in attitude, for they did not come up the hard way. Steve Davis, who became world champion at the age of twenty-three, probably has the best outlook, but I hope we do not price ourselves out of the exhibition game market. I know it would be better in some ways for the top professional to prepare himself for the big tournaments and cut out the exhibitions and travelling, which would reduce the strain a good deal, but the clubs are part of the life I love.

One of the favourites is a small place in the mountains of Wales, in the west at Llandysul, where I first went ten years ago at the invitation of Vernon Williams. This club has room for only 140 or 150 spectators and most of them are not young any more. After the snooker we go upstairs to have tea off trestle tables covered in white paper. Round come the sandwiches and home-baked cakes. It is really delightful. I hope we will always be flexible in the matter of fees, for making a journey to play in a club like that is very much worthwhile.

I am not overlooking the fact that such trips are a different proposition now than when I first started my rounds. My accounts show that in 1969 I was only charging a little over £5 for eighteen gallons of petrol. Meals on a visit to Kent were billed at less than £1.

Not that I make a practice of looking back rather than ahead. I have my eyes on a seventh world title and I hope to play a part in developing snooker in every country. It is a game with a universal appeal and I hope that one day every lad and every girl of every nationality will have the chance that I had to climb out of the pits to the top of the world.

APPENDIX

Career Highlights

Amateur champion of Wales: 1950, 1951, 1952, 1953, 1954, 1955

Great Britain Police champion: 1962, 1963, 1965, 1966

English amateur champion: 1964

Club and Institute Union champion: 1965

With Jonathan Barron won a Test series in South Africa 2–1 in 1967

BBC Television Pot Black champion: 1969 and 1979

World professional champion: 1970, 1973, 1974, 1975, 1976 and 1978

Won the Park Drive £600 and £2,000 tournaments: 1972

Helped Great Britain to beat the Rest of the World: 1973

Won the Pontins professional tournament: 1974; the professional and open in 1975; and the professional in 1976

Won the Watney Mann tournament: 1974

Won the Irish title: 1975

Won the Benson and Hedges tournament: 1976

Won the William Hill championship of Wales: 1977

Won the Daily Mirror Champion of Champions tournament at Wembley: 1978

Captained Wales to victory in the State Express World Cup team championship tournaments of 1979 and 1980